"My friend Chuck puts into words so many of the things I've been trying to verbalize and process as a pastor in our current world. In a culture where so much is constantly changing, why is it that so often the Church fails to adapt? In Pivot Now, Chuck challenges leaders—in every area of ministry—to take the hard steps to meet people where they're at today. Yes, the truths of the Gospel will never change, but the moment we're living in undoubtedly has. If as pastors and leaders we want to continue reaching people into the next decade and beyond, Pivot Now should be required reading."
- *Adam Weber, lead pastor of Embrace Church, author, podcast host*

"Pivot Now is a timely call for church leaders serving and navigating communities through the complexities of our day. Chuck Bomar gives language to the disorientation so many of us feel and helps us see the landscape with renewed courage and compassion. This isn't another book of change for change's sake but a deep invitation to hold fast to the way of Jesus while adapting methods for the sake of the mission. Pivot Now is a helpful guide for leaders who desire to serve faithfully and effectively."
- *Jay Y. Kim, Pastor and Author*

"In basketball, to pivot means one foot remains constant while the other moves to adapt to the situation to create a better path to success. Exactly what Chuck has created in this work for ministry leaders. Incredible insights around a pivot posture. The art of expecting, understanding, embracing even celebrating change while remaining anchored in biblical foundational truths and values. From beginning to end I was encouraged and challenged to reshape the way I think of change. Mission over methods!"

- Shane Williamson, President and CEO Fellowship of Christian Athletes

"Pivot Now is a book that is not theoretical about leadership and change. It comes from someone who has been in the trenches of leading through the ups and downs and fast-changing world we are in, which requires quick, but deep thinking and the ability to pivot. I say this not as cliche, but when Chuck Bomar speaks about leadership and mission, I listen - and Pivot Now is both extremely helpful to listen to and also has much to actually put into practice as it teaches us."

- Dan Kimball, Pastor, Professor, and Author

PIVOT NOW

Mastering Change for the Sake of Our Mission

By

CHUCK BOMAR

This book is dedicated to my family.

The amount of change we have gone through together is immense.

Barbara:
Your unconditional love has steadied me during some of the rockiest
moments of life. It's not an exaggeration to say you have been the
backbone to our family. I am beyond grateful to live alongside you.
I'd choose you again and again and again.

Karis, Hope and Sayla:
God knew I needed you. God has used you to change and grow me in
ways I'm still amazed by. Being your father and watching you change
and mature has been my greatest joy.
You are loved.

CONTENTS

Start Here

Too many ministry leaders are experiencing a kind of weariness sleep doesn't fix. And much of it comes from trying to lead through changes they can't yet name. I know this all too well.

I started in ministry as a camp counselor.
Actually, I was just a warm body.

A junior high pastor needed an extra adult. You know the drill: stay awake and make sure nobody gets hurt.

I fit the description. I showed up.

That accidental beginning launched me into more than thirty years of church-based ministry I never saw coming.

Some of the best moments of my life happened in these years. Some of the hardest did too.

From that summer camp I became an intern, then a youth pastor, then spent nearly a decade as a "NextGen" pastor, mainly focusing on college ministry. I planted a church in Portland with almost no connections and led it for twelve years. I've led a doctoral program in Contextual Leadership and have helped dozens of organizations navigate seasons of disruption and change. I've built teams, navigated board conflict, counseled couples for years only to see marriages still fall apart. I think I've experienced both the highest highs and lowest lows of ministry.

Across all of it one realization kept surfacing:

I've spent my life inside change.

I was born into it.
I've lived through it.
Led through it.
I've been hurt by it.
Created it in ways that unfortunately hurt others.

But at the end of the day, I'm a Church guy.
I love the Church.
I serve as an elder, teach, and still believe the local church is God's primary instrument of transformation in the world.

That's why I'm writing this book. Because I believe staying the same might be the greatest threat facing the Church today.

Not because leaders don't care.
Not because churches aren't trying.
It's because the landscape has shifted beneath our feet and many

of us haven't adjusted our footing. Feeling the changes but not naming them only adds to the exhaustion.

I've sensed it for years. We're missing where people are.
Not intentionally.
Not lazily.
But structurally.

The assumptions we once made about faith, discipleship, belonging, and authority no longer hold. The way people process faith has changed dramatically and it is now creating an unprecedented need for change in how we approach our mission.

We feel the changes, but where do we start?

It begins with pivoting. The very definition is a central point on which everything turns and it signifies adaptability, allowing organizations to shift strategies in response to new information.

So, let me be clear: I'm not calling for a massive overhaul. Many leaders are already tired, and this isn't about throwing out what's working in our ministries.

But there are specific and significant ways we must adapt if we are to move forward faithfully in a changing landscape. If we don't, the weariness deepens and the mission begins to erode. My goal in the following pages is to first help articulate what is happening because, as I will say again, we can't pivot toward what we don't understand.

But, before we go further, I need to say something: change has never been theoretical for me and my family. It's been deeply personal.

It begins with both of my grandfathers. Both my mom and dad had rough childhoods where their dads suddenly abandoned the family when they were young. That type of change cuts deep.

For my mom, this early pain contributed to her being divorced twice with two kids by the age of 23. She is a survivor and one of the strongest people I know. She did what she needed to do to raise us, which meant we moved whenever rent rose or relationships fell apart. Before my senior year of high school I had lived in eleven homes across seven cities. Change was the norm for us.

People often ask if moving all the time was hard on me. The honest answer is no, it wasn't. Not having my dad around was hard. But the change itself? That felt normal. I came home from visiting my stepdad one weekend to find we had moved to a completely different house. I didn't even know we were moving. Change was just how life worked.

I learned to adapt. It was survival.

And now, what was once instability has become something of a gift.

Over time I've been able to sense change when it's needed. I can usually articulate it earlier than most when it surfaces. It's likely why I can buy struggling companies with the hope of actually turning them around. It's why I can consult for companies and churches and help them get unstuck.

It's not because I'm special.
It's because change is what I've always known.

Change doesn't scare me. Standing still does more so.

That's why I'm writing this book.

Not to chase trends.
Not to abandon conviction or solid theology.
Not to change for change's sake.

This book is about protecting our mission by articulating what has changed, understanding a leadership mindset for change and then stating some very specific ways change is needed. That's the flow of the book.

It's about naming what has happened to the people sitting in our churches, scrolling past our content, and walking through our neighborhoods. It's about looking at research as a tool for

adjusting our approach so the unchanging gospel can reach a
rapidly changing world.

Because here's the statement that drives me:
God's mission will outlast the methods we love.

And here is the question that haunts me:

If we want to see people and our communities change, why
would we be resistant to evaluating or changing ourselves?

And here is a question you might consider:
What if the very methods fueling your growth today are the ones
that quietly limit your impact tomorrow?

You see, we are no longer preaching or leading in a shared
reality. Algorithms curate identity. Echo chambers shape
worldviews. Belonging is chosen cautiously. Authority is
questioned instinctively. Change is occurring at warp speed.

The gap between church and culture isn't just theological.

It's cognitive.
Relational.
Structural.

This book is an attempt to help bridge the gap by giving you words to describe what you likely feel. Then, to give you steps to consider as you seek to protect the mission.

There is a lifecycle to every ministry. But if a ministry dies in our lifetime, let it not be because we refused to pivot.

The mission hasn't changed. But the moment has.

And it calls for leaders who are ready —
ready to listen,
ready to learn,
ready to lead,
ready to pivot.

What Has Changed?

"Forget the former things. Do not dwell on the past. See, I am doing a new thing. Now it springs up, do you not perceive it? I am making a way in the wilderness and streams in the wasteland."

— Isaiah 43:18-19

1: Change Is Always the Same

Change has always been the same.

It's constant.

It always creates fear and especially when we can't name it.

It always forces us to decide what to keep, and what to release.

It's the same.

Think about the major shifts in civilization. The agricultural revolution reshaped how people lived and organized their lives. The printing press changed how truth and ideas spread. The industrial revolution reordered economies, families, and entire societies. The digital revolution has done the same in our lifetime.

Every generation has faced massive cultural shifts. And every generation has had people who resisted those shifts with everything they had.

I'm old enough to remember when the internet felt threatening. We didn't know its impact on us. It felt distant, disruptive, and hard to grasp.

Social media followed the same path. It was feared at first, and yet now has become the most powerful communication and marketing force in human history.

The same with the unknowns around artificial intelligence tools.

Because when we don't understand change, we don't know how it will affect us. And uncertainty always breeds fear.

The Church is no exception. Culture has always been shifting around the people of God. Ancient Israel navigated change within its own history. The early church wrestled through the transition from Jewish to Gentile contexts, discerning what to hold and what to release. The Reformation reshaped how millions understood their relationship with God. The Great Awakenings transformed religious practice across America.

Change has always been part of our story.

But we all know the pace of it has accelerated.
Dramatically.

What once unfolded over generations now happens in years. What once took years now happens in months.

Previous generations could adapt without feeling like the ground was constantly moving beneath them.

Today, change comes much faster than we can process it.

Which means navigating this moment requires a new posture. We can't just respond to change once it arrives. We must become ready before we even know what's coming.

We all sense the changes.

The challenge is articulating it and learning to pivot wisely.

The Echo Chamber Age

In the last decade alone, the way people process information has been revolutionized. But it's not just the speed and accessibility to information that has changed.

It's the way it's fed to us.

Social media algorithms have created something that didn't exist before: personalized echo chambers that reinforce whatever you already believe, while filtering out everything else.

This has changed how people hear, process, and respond to truth.

Think about how this works.

You are being sold.

That's the business model of social media platforms. Facebook, Instagram, TikTok. All of them sell your attention to advertisers. Your value increases the more you stay engaged.

What keeps you engaged?
Content that holds your attention.
What holds your attention most?
Content that confirms what you already think.

This means your engagement takes priority over what is actually true. Platforms work to reinforce "your truth." This is called *algorithmic curation*. It creates a self-reinforcing loop that matches your interests and beliefs. It's brilliant marketing. And it has fundamentally reshaped how people process information.

Any challenging views, alternative perspectives, or diverse information are filtered out of your feeds.

Because, your frustration leads to disengagement.
And your disengagement lowers your value.

So everything is centered on what you agree with or are already interested in. Content is curated to match what *you* want.

So, now it's not *social* media as much as it is *interest* media.

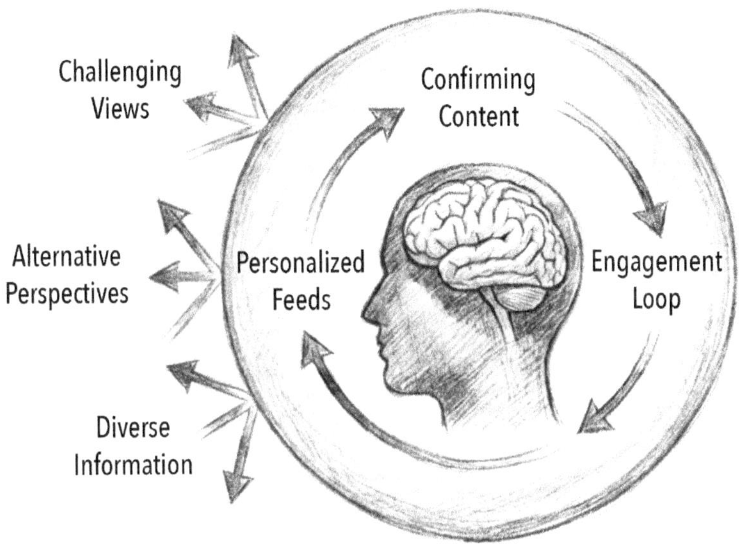

If you watch a video about watches, you'll start seeing more watch content. If you engage with right-leaning political content, you'll see more of that. If you engage with left-leaning content, same thing. You don't have to do anything intentional. The algorithm is doing the work, quietly sorting you into an echo chamber where your existing views and interests are amplified back to you while opposing views are filtered out.

This way you stay engaged.
And yet, become disconnected at the same time.

The result is that we end up living in polarized realities. People exist in completely different information ecosystems, all convinced that anyone who disagrees with them is misinformed or misguided. This is especially true with politics, but it extends far beyond that. People are only seeing pieces of the picture that align with their existing views. They're only seeing what the algorithm decides will keep them engaged.

The algorithm isn't trying to determine what is true.

And yet, everyone feels fully informed.
Everyone feels confident in their perspective.
Everyone feels like they see clearly.

This has profound implications. It's not just politics that gets filtered through echo chambers. It's theology. It's ethics. It's how people understand church, Scripture, and what it means to follow Jesus. People are forming beliefs in environments designed to confirm rather than challenge, to reinforce rather than refine.

It's why conversations across differences feel increasingly impossible. Everything people consume online aligns with what they already believe. If something challenges them, they disengage and retreat back into the comfort of their echo chamber. It's more peaceful that way. There is little to no capacity for challenge or disagreement.
It's how we operate now.
It's part of how we've been formed.

But here's what this means for ministry leaders:
You are no longer trying to reach a shared reality.

Every person sitting in front of you is now living in a different information universe. They are not neutral listeners. They are pre-formed.

This means you may think you're teaching one message, but it's actually being heard through hundreds of curated realities at once. The daily content designed to keep them engaged, shapes how they hear everything you say too. And they have limited resilience to hear something they don't already agree with.

There was a time when a pastor could assume a shared baseline. A shared moral language. A shared understanding of truth. A shared respect for Scripture. A shared cultural framework for understanding the world. That world is gone.

Today, two people sitting next to each other in your church may not agree on what is true, what is good, what authority means, or even what the gospel is. We can no longer think they are starting from the same place. We can't assume they are part of the same formation chamber.

We are no longer speaking into a shared framework of meaning. We are speaking into hundreds of curated realities at once.

This changes what preaching does,
what leadership requires, and
how discipleship must be structured.

Otherwise, our ministries can remain biblically faithful and still
be functionally ineffective. Not because truth has lost its power.
But because people are no longer hearing that truth within a
shared understanding of reality.

This is the core problem: our leadership, preaching and
discipleship models often operate as if we are living in a shared
reality. That's an illusion.

Clarity must increase.
Intentionality must increase.
Empathy must increase.

Because if we don't understand how people are processing
information, we will keep applying yesterday's methods to
today's reality. Speaking clearly and wondering why people aren't
changing. Wondering why transformation feels elusive.

The world we now lead in is:
fragmented,
personalized,
decentralized.

And if we don't understand what this has produced, we will misdiagnose the moment.

Because echo chambers have not just changed how people receive information. They have changed how people assemble faith itself.

Which means old frameworks won't carry the mission forward.

Institutional Inertia

Here's the tension we now face:

When algorithm-shaped formation accelerates culture while the Church adapts at glacial speed, a dangerous gap widens between us and the people we're called to reach.

This is the gap where the mission quietly erodes. And if we're honest, many of us haven't adapted well. Inertia—the tendency to avoid change—in the Church is a hindrance for mission.

Part of the problem is clarity.
You can't pivot toward what you don't understand. When we struggle to articulate what is happening, we freeze.

Part of the problem is training.
Most ministry preparation teaches us how to shepherd the present, not necessarily how to lead into the future.

And part of the problem is emotional.

Churches are built to preserve truth. Change can feel like compromise to us, even when it's necessary for our mission.

I understand those tensions, however, the challenge before us is not choosing between faithfulness and adaptation. It is recognizing that adapting is the very expression of faithfulness.

God's mission will outlive the methods we love.

It always has.

It always will.

This leads us to a hard but necessary question:

What if the biggest threat to your ministry isn't change — but staying the same?

This is hard to answer. We are stewards of ancient truth. We are called to preserve what must never change. We are not supposed to bend every time culture shifts. There is wisdom in both caution and stability. Some ministries are very fruitful.

But there is also danger in avoiding the question.

Because over time, we can begin to confuse the truth we preserve with the methods we prefer. We can start treating our communication styles, structures, and assumptions as if they are sacred when they are simply a familiar model.

And when that happens, we don't just preserve the message.
We fossilize it.

The gospel remains as powerful as ever, but it must be delivered in ways people recognize as meaningful. We must guard the mission by reshaping our methods because if not, protecting our methods will quietly become our mission.

Mission doesn't die because culture shifts.
Mission dies when leaders refuse to pivot toward it.

Imagine a church planted forty years ago. The language, assumptions, and ministry strategies that once connected deeply with its community made perfect sense in their time. But if those same methods remain unchanged while everything around them has shifted, should we be surprised if the church begins to struggle reaching people?

When methods remain static in a rapidly changing world, even faithful churches can slowly drift from effectiveness. It's not because they lose their grip on the truth. They lost the practice of cutting away things that no longer bear fruit. John 15:2 comes to mind.

We must be anchored and adaptive at the same time.
Rooted in orthodoxy.
Responsive in mission.

Our goal is to hold tightly to what must never change while holding loosely to everything that can.

This is not easy. The fear of getting it wrong often paralyzes us into doing nothing at all. We ask endless questions. We debate endlessly. Put together committee's. We inevitably critique culture from a distance. We wait for clarity that rarely comes. And while we wait, the gap widens.

In the short term, resisting change can feel safer.
In the long term, it quietly undermines our calling.

Because a mission without change becomes a seed that never grows.

The goal of this book is not to push you toward change for change's sake. It's to help you discern what must remain anchored and what must be adjusted so the mission can move forward in your context.

If we are going to lead faithfully in an echo chamber world, we must learn to pivot without drifting.
To adapt without compromising.
To change methods while preserving the message.

And that begins with understanding just how deeply the landscape has shifted.

Can't Pivot Toward What You Can't See

I've watched this happen again and again over the last thirty years.

Churches that were once thriving slowly became stagnant. Not because they stopped caring about people, but because they stopped recognizing change and evaluating their methods.

They held tightly to the truth.
But they also held tightly to methods.
And eventually, they couldn't tell the difference[1].

Every church the apostle Paul planted has died.
Churches have life cycles. We know that.

But a church slowly losing its mission because leaders refuse to acknowledge reality seems different. Refusing to change isn't inevitable. It's preventable.

When leaders get stuck in their ways, it's rarely because they don't love God or care about people. It's usually because they haven't clearly named what has changed around them. And when change remains undefined, it quietly produces fear. Fear leads to hesitation. Hesitation leads to drift.

---

[1] Matthew 7:8-9

This is why clarity matters before strategy.
Understanding must come before adjustment.

I believe if we can articulate what is actually happening around us, we can lead like missionaries again. It will allow us to adjust our posture, our language, and our methods to meet people where they really are, not where we assume they are.

Because we cannot pivot toward what we don't understand.

So, before we talk about adapting our preaching...
Before we talk about our leadership mindset...
Before we rethink discipleship structures...

We have to understand the landscape. Understanding how algorithmic-curation has shaped how we process is a start. But we must understand more of its impact.

Because once you see it, you won't be able to unsee it.

Every chapter in this book is paired with a companion video. Scan the QR code below to access them for free.

2: The Decoupled Network

I experienced a "pivot now" moment during a Zoom call.

At the time, I was serving as President/COO of The Barna Group. I had stepped in to help the organization navigate transition, but I was also energized by the opportunity to help create resources that would genuinely serve churches. That has always been the heart of Barna, and I was honored to come alongside in that work.

Once I got settled, I realized just how much insight lived inside the organization. Decades of research. Mountains of data. Over forty years tracking how people relate to faith, belief, church, and culture. It was both fascinating and overwhelming.

But, for me, the pivot moment didn't come from reports.

It came from a conversation.

One of the people I respect most at Barna is the VP of research, Daniel Copeland. He has a rare ability to see patterns most of us miss and to explain complex cultural shifts with striking clarity.

During one of our weekly Zoom calls, we were discussing trends in data he was looking at. We were discussing how some of the findings seemed contradictory at first glance. But Daniel saw something else entirely. He said although the data seemed conflicting, it was revealing a shift in how people were processing faith itself.

Then he used a phrase I had never heard before.

"The decoupling of faith."

It felt like someone turned on a light in a dark room I'd been stumbling around in for years. I had been sensing the shifts. Feeling the contradictions. Experiencing the gap between how churches were communicating and how people were actually processing belief.

I just didn't have language for it.

Until that moment.

Daniel wasn't just naming a trend. He was describing a structural change in how faith works in people's lives. And once I saw it, I couldn't unsee it.

Things hadn't just changed, they had fundamentally reorganized. That's the moment I started my journey to writing this book.

The Four Dimensions

To understand the significance of the shift toward a decoupled faith, we first need to understand what *used to be*.

I'll lay this out because this will serve as the foundation for our practical application throughout the book.

Historically, Christianity has been understood through four core dimensions: identity, beliefs, practices, and affiliations. These categories have been described in different ways over time, but the basic framework has remained remarkably consistent. Together, they form the fabric of how someone understands and relates to the Christian faith, or any faith, for that matter.

It's historically been understood as starting with how we identify ourselves, and then it flows outward from there.

The dimension of *identity* answers the question, *Who am I?* It's how a person understands themselves at the deepest level. When someone identifies as a Christian, they're making a claim about how they interpret the world, how they make decisions, and how they relate to others. Identity shapes everything else and how we go about this creates either confusion or resilience.

Beliefs are what people hold to be true. This includes what they believe about God, humanity, morality, and sacred tradition. Beliefs form the internal framework through which life is interpreted. They shape identity and give direction to behavior.

Practices are what people actually do with their identity and beliefs. They are where faith becomes visible. Christianity isn't just about what we believe; it's about how belief becomes embodied. Historically, practices like gathering with the church, reading Scripture, prayer, and serving others have been the tangible expressions of Christian life. This is where convictions showed up in real life.

Affiliations are the relational circles people find a sense of belonging. It's who they gather with, what institutions they support, and what communities they identify with. Historically, this often showed up through denominational life. You were Baptist, Methodist, Lutheran, Catholic. Your affiliation told people where you belonged and, in many ways, what you believed and how you lived.

For most of Christian history in America these four dimensions were seen as built on each other in a predictable sequence.

Identity framed out beliefs.
Beliefs led to certain practices.
Practices then crystalized as affiliations.

If you identified as a Christian, that meant you aligned with certain beliefs. Those beliefs naturally expressed themselves through practices like church attendance, prayer, Scripture reading, generosity, evangelism. And those shared practices were organized through affiliation. You joined a church. You became part of a denomination. You belonged to a community that reinforced your identity and beliefs.

Everything was connected. Integrated. Reinforcing one another.

For decades, leaders used this model to understand how the dimensions practically functioned. It worked because the manner and speed of information allowed for such a layered approach to faith.

It was simple. Predictable. Coherent.
And leaders used it as a guide to move people toward a mission.

But, that model doesn't capture the complexities of today. Faith isn't layered in that way anymore.

And once that breaks apart, how we lead, preach, and disciple must be reconsidered. Remember: methods are to be held loosely. They are not doctrine.

The Decoupled Network

Decoupling describes how each dimension of faith is now processed independently from the others. Rather than seeing concentric circles forming a layered identity, we should now see it as a network or massive web.

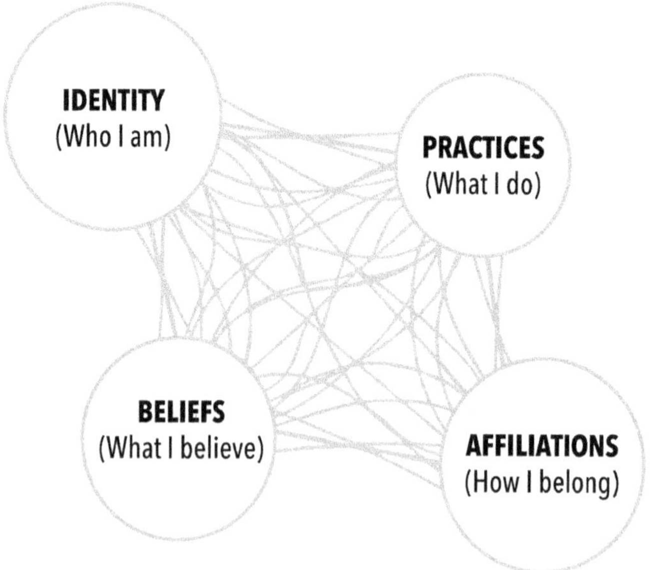

This means the way the dimensions connect differs from person to person. They may still connect, but we can no longer assume they do. The connections are no longer predictable or sequential.

You hear it in everyday conversation.

Someone might say, "I like Jesus but not the Church." Belief is decoupled from affiliation and practice.

Another person hesitates to identify as "evangelical," yet holds deeply to convictions historically associated with that label. Identity is decoupled from beliefs.

Some engage in traditional Christian practices but don't hold core Christian beliefs about Jesus.

Others don't identify as Christian at all but have strong opinions about what Christians should believe or how they should behave. You'll even find people who feel affiliated with a church but aren't sure they believe what it teaches.

It's all over the place. It's a complex network. A web.

That's the point. The dimensions that once moved together now float freely, each processed independently. They may still connect, but how they connect varies from person to person. People assemble and curate their own configuration of identity, belief, practice, and belonging.

That's what *algorithmic curation* has ingrained in us.

From a layered model it feels contradictory or hypocritical, but once we understand decoupling it's much more effective to see it as complexity rather than contradiction.

And, yet, it gets even more complex.

Not only are the dimensions separating from one another, each dimension is also fragmenting within itself. Some elements have remained relatively stable over time, but others are evolving in ways previously unseen.

We're not just dealing with separation between the dimensions. We're dealing with how they are re-forming within themselves. So, the best way to see what is true about how people are processing faith today looks more like this:

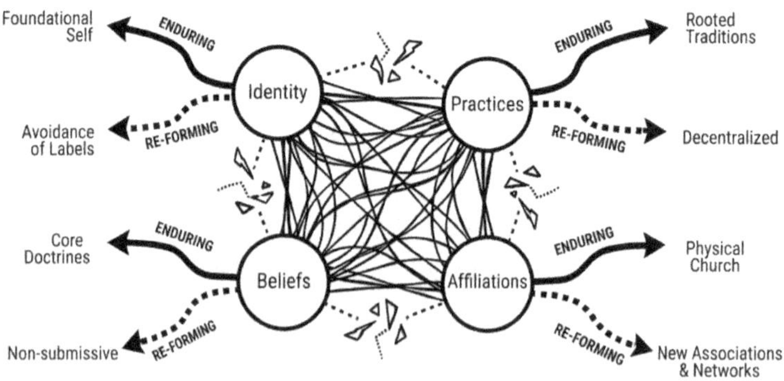

This complexity creates the leadership challenge in front of us.

Putting The Pieces Together

It took me a while to process this and to be fair Daniel was still processing too. But over time the picture began to settle for me.

This new reality requires the Church to pivot.
It's too big to avoid.

Here's my best attempt to summarize the landscape we are navigating from a pastoral perspective:

Every heart experiences faith at its own rhythm. Modern faith is a web of connections between floating dimensions, each fragmenting on its own timeline and in its own self-inflicted direction. People are assembling their faith in ways that lack coherence to outsiders and sometimes even to themselves.

Faith processing has become highly individualized.
Mostly non-submissive to outside sources.
Increasingly self-directed.

Which means the self is enthroned, quietly reigning at the center of the faith process — in an unprecedented way.

There are many factors contributing to this shift. The echo chamber reality of the digital world is core to it. Social media fragments ideas, reinforces beliefs, and centers everything around the individual's comfort. However, whether algorithmic curation caused this fragmentation or simply revealed it is worth some discussion. But the conclusion remains the same:

Things are now fundamentally different.
And it requires a new level of clarity from us as leaders.
Our layered model may have worked before. It doesn't now.

If you're a pastor preaching on Sunday morning, you might assume you're speaking to a room full of Christians who share a common understanding of the words you use.

But you're not.

You might assume if you teach proper doctrine people will then naturally implement it into how they define themselves (identity) and what they do (practices). Or, you might assume if you lean more practical in your teaching that people will connect it with what they believe.

But we must recognize those assumptions are based on a layered model of understanding how faith is processed. Now, the entire process is decoupled and re-forming, not layered.

You're speaking to a room of people processing the four dimensions independently from one another, at different paces, with different priorities and often even different definitions around them.

Faith is processed from entirely different echo chambers.

Some are primarily wrestling with identity.
They're asking, *Who am I?*
They're unsure whether "Christian" is even a label they want.
This goes beyond semantic drift. It reflects a deeper shift in how people locate themselves in the world.

Others are focused on belief.
They're trying to determine what's actually true and whether the church can be trusted. But even belief itself is splintering, shaped by competing voices and generational differences.

Others are focused on practice.
They want to know what to do and how to live. Some are trying to connect belief to behavior. Others rely on practice to compensate for uncertainty about belief. Still others use practice to manage guilt or create a sense of spiritual control.

And some are simply searching for belonging.
They're not starting with doctrine or discipline. They're looking for community. A place to be known, first. A place to fit. How they evaluate whether your church can offer that is deeply personal and maybe even subconscious.

The key is to recognize that people aren't processing these in layers. They don't automatically connect anymore. The layered model sees this as being hypocritical. How can you say you're a Christian and feel totally free to live with your partner outside of marriage? How can you say you believe in Jesus and never give to kingdom work?

It's simple: each dimension is decoupled from the others. How you identify doesn't automatically connect to what you say you believe or do anymore. What you believe doesn't naturally flow into how you connect to the community of Christ.

So, again, while the layered identity would say this doesn't make sense, the decoupled network understands all of it as normal faith processing. People are processing one or maybe two dimensions at a time, separately from the other dimensions.

Understanding the four dimension reality and the decoupled network doesn't solve everything. But it helps us articulate what is actually happening and see what we're actually dealing with — a non-linear faith process we must address.

It gives language to the complexity many leaders feel but struggle to define. It helps us identify where to focus our leadership, preaching, and discipleship efforts. And it gives us a framework for engaging people where they actually are rather than where we assume them to be.

Clarity always precedes movement.

Because you can't pivot toward what you can't name.

So, before we move into practical leadership implications, we need to spend a little more time understanding what is actually happening within each dimension.

Let's now turn to how they are re-forming, according to the research.

3: A Re-Formation Era

Yesterday's assumptions can't solve today's ministry problems.

By now you are beginning to see the reality: the faith landscape has changed. The four dimensions of faith are no longer predictable. They're splintering and decentralizing.

This is important because, again, when change is hard to define, it creates fear. And fear freezes movement for leaders, which is dangerous because mission drift begins the moment courage pauses.

Staying put may feel safe in the moment, but it slowly erodes mission over time. So if we want to lead faithfully, we have to see today clearly so that we can pivot confidently.

We now know the four dimensions (identity, beliefs, practices, and affiliation) not only operate independently, but each is evolving internally within itself. Multiple changes, happening simultaneously, and often in contradictory ways that are unpredictable.

This is the complexity.
We are in the midst of a great Re-formation.

Anchored To Mission

Mission drift is never accidental nor does it explode on us. It's cumulative. It happens one delayed decision at a time. We must gain a deeper understanding of what endures and what is re-forming within these dimensions if faithfulness to our mission matters.

When we talk about what's *enduring*, we are referring to certain beliefs, practices, and longings that remain steady across generations. These might be seen as some of the anchors of faith, the truths and rhythms that have formed Christians for centuries and continue to do so.

But the defining story of today is really what's re-forming.

These are the new expressions, fractures, and shifts taking shape in real time. Things that once moved together are now splintering into new patterns we can articulate. Faith is still present, but it's operating differently.

If we're honest, far more seems to be re-forming than enduring. And leaders who ignore that will keep feeling disoriented as they try to apply yesterday's methods to a world that no longer responds to them.

Holding both *enduring* and *re-forming* realities together is essential. Lose that tension, and you lose touch with what's actually happening.

If you *only* see what's enduring, you'll assume stability where there is actually change. You'll keep using familiar methods long after they've stopped reaching people.

If you *only* see what's re-forming, you'll lose heart. Everything can feel unstable, overwhelming, and impossible to navigate. Leaders who live here often either retreat into nostalgia where you lament needed change or you'll experience a pessimism that ends in paralysis.

But *ignoring* what's re-forming is just as dangerous. Every initiative risks misfiring. Opportunities pass unnoticed. A harvest can stand unattended while you keep working fields that no longer produce.

I think of a three-cord strand as the best way of staying anchored to our mission.

Gospel truth is the core strand. Then ...

one strand is what endures and ...

the other is what is re-forming.

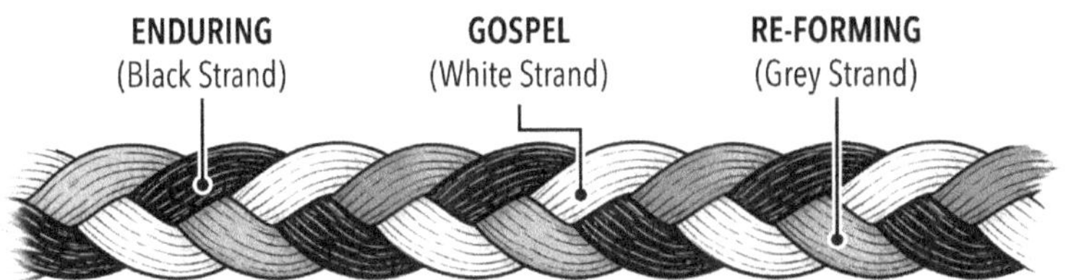

Keeping all three in tension is really what keeps us anchored to the mission. Lose either strand, and drift begins.

Mission drift is never accidental.

So the real question is: Will our leadership remain anchored while adaptive or will fear cause us to lose our footing?

Because although faith is not disappearing.
It is definitely decentralizing.

Looking At Research

One of the dangers of research is that we often find it fascinating but not formative. We see a new statistic and think, *That's interesting.*

And then we move on.

The information never makes its way into our leadership, or our discipleship models. We may quote Barna in a sermon, but the reality is it stays in the category of insight but never becomes instruction.

That's the danger of this chapter.

If the data only makes us curious without making us courageous, we've missed the point.

When you look across research published over the last five years or so, you don't just see trends. You see faith re-forming in real time. There is movement, fragmentation, and entirely new patterns of identity, belief, practice, and affiliation taking shape.[2]

And it's happening across all four dimensions at once.

Yes, some things endure.
But far more is changing than staying the same.

Information without application leads to irrelevance so having the courage to evaluate what you are doing matters. I encourage you to really process how this may require change in your context.

---

[2] For a fuller list of sources considered for this study and direct links see QR code at end of chapter.

But, we also know that understanding is the first step. That's why, before we talk about strategy, we need to see the landscape even more clearly. With some specifics.

Let's walk through each dimension so we can specifically name what is actually re-forming right in front of us.

Identity: steady, yet re-forming

When it comes to what's enduring within Christian identity, Christianity still remains the dominant self-proclaimed religious identity in the United States.[3] Despite headlines about decline, the total number of people who identify as Christian has remained relatively stable.[4] In some segments, especially among younger men, personal commitment to follow Jesus is even rising.[5]

---

[3] Pew Research Center, "America's Changing Religious Landscape," May 12, 2015, updated analysis and datasets: Pew finds Christianity remains the largest self-identified religious category in the United States, even amid long-term decline. The total number of Americans identifying as Christian has remained substantial due to population growth and generational replacement.

[4] Barna research indicates the proportion of U.S. adults identifying as Christian has remained near two-thirds. Barna, "What Does It Mean When People Say They Are 'Christian'?" or "Most Americans Identify as Christian" in the 2018 State of Church report.

[5] Institute for Family Studies, "Young Men and Religious Commitment," analysis of national survey data (2023): Reports signs of renewed religious interest among younger men in certain segments, including increased openness to faith identity, participation, and commitment compared to previous cohorts.

But the meaning of that identity is changing.

The label *Christian* is no longer a reliable indicator of spiritual conviction, theological alignment, or engagement with historic Christian practices.[6] Some who claim the identity have little connection to Christ, while others who reject traditional labels like "evangelical" demonstrate deep commitment to how that word has been traditionally defined.

At the same time, a growing number of adults express commitment to Jesus while distancing themselves from institutional church involvement.[7] Among Gen Z especially, belonging is being redefined as spiritually open, but institutionally detached.[8]

Identity is increasingly shaped by personal desire rather than submission to shared doctrine or programmatic formation.[9]

------

[6] Barna Group, "Americans Remain Spiritually Active, but Biblical Worldview Is Waning," Barna.com. This tracking research indicates that while many Americans, including self-identified Christians, continue to engage in spiritual practices, their beliefs are often inconsistent and lack a coherent biblical worldview, complicating how Christian identity is understood and lived.

[7] *Self-Described Christians Dominate America but Wrestle with Four Aspects of Spiritual Depth*, Barna.com, accessed December 20, 2025

[8] *Faith in Flux: Changes in Religious Identity and Practice*, Barna.com

[9] *Spiritually Open but Not Religious: How Americans Are Reimagining Faith*, Barna.com, Documents the growing segment of Americans who remain spiritually curious and engaged while distancing themselves from institutional religion and traditional labels.

So although Christian identity isn't necessarily declining.
It is being re-formed and redefined in an individualized way.

And recognizing that shift matters for leadership. When people
are curating their own sense of identity, what we say matters. For
example, phrases like, "You have a personal relationship with
Jesus" can be heard in a variety of ways that only serve the
enthronement of self. It's a true statement, but rethinking our
context may cause us to shift how we talk about faith.

We will discuss this further, but this is why we seek clarity first.
Because in order for us to pivot wisely, we have to understand
why.

Beliefs: respected, yet re-forming

Beliefs show the same pattern.

What's enduring: most Americans still express belief in the God
of the bible.[10] Jesus, spirituality, and the Bible continue to hold

---

[10] Pew Research Center, "When Americans Say They Believe in God, What Do
They Mean?" April 25, 2018: Finds that belief in God remains widespread in the
U.S., though definitions and theological clarity vary significantly across
individuals and traditions.

high levels of respect, even among non-Christians.[11] These foundations haven't disappeared.[12]

But how belief itself is being processed is shifting.

The decoupled reality has led to fewer Christians saying their faith shapes their daily decisions.[13] Fewer feel responsible to share it.[14] The Bible's authority is no longer assumed, even among Christians,[15] and beliefs around morality, sexuality, and social issues vary widely across generations and communities.[16]

For many younger adults, belief is no longer anchored primarily in orthodox doctrine, but more so in their experience.[17] It is

---

[11] "Religious and Spiritual Beliefs: Belief in God or a Universal Spirit and Certainty of Belief," *PewResearch.org*, February 26, 2025. Also see: "Belief in God in U.S. Dips to 81%, a New Low," *Gallup.com*, June 17, 2022

[12] Public Religion Research Institute, *"American Values Atlas—Religious Beliefs Trends"*: PRRI data shows enduring spiritual belief across generations, even among those less connected to institutional religion.

[13] *The State of the Church 2023: Fewer Practicing Christians See Faith as Central to Daily Life*, Barna.com

[14] *Christians Are Hesitant to Share Their Faith—Especially Younger Generations*, Barna.com— Shows a continued decrease in the number of Christians who feel personally responsible to share their faith, with sharp generational differences.

[15] *What Americans Believe About the Bible*, Barna.com— Finds declining belief in the Bible's divine authority and factual accuracy, including among self-identified Christians.

[16] *Faith and Sexuality: Where Christians Agree—and Don't*, Barna.com — Highlights internal divisions among Christians on sexuality, moral authority, and social ethics.

[17] *What Does It Mean to Be Spiritually Open?*, Barna.com, June 21, 2023

evaluated by its impact: whether it does good, carries meaning, and helps people flourish. They are drawn to faith that feels honest and embodied, not merely certain and well-defined.[18] This is substantially different from older generations who had a more layered reality.

This creates a different landscape for leaders. A decoupled one.

What once sounded clear can now sound muddy, even contradictory. What felt sure now feels optional.

The risk is treating this as interesting rather than formative. Data can't just stay interesting. It has to become instructive.

Because, for instance, when belief shifts but our language doesn't, communication misfires. We assume shared definitions that no longer exist, we preach in ways people don't feel. Or when someone's faith processes are decoupled we can become frustrated and condemning rather than helpful to them.

Respect for belief is still high.
Submission to belief is not.

— Defines "spiritual openness" and shows that many Americans—including younger generations—express curiosity, exploration, and an openness to spiritual realities even outside traditional religious labels.

[18] *Gen Z: 5 Things You Need to Know About Gen Z (Vol. 3), Barna.com,* September 12, 2024 — Highlights how Gen Z navigates identity, morality, and faith, demonstrating their unique pathways to meaning and belonging that do not always align with institutional religious categories.

And that gap changes how we lead, how we preach, and how we disciple. This is why pivoting is to be seen as faithfulness and standing still no longer makes sense.

Practices: present, yet re-forming

Practices reveal a similar pattern.

What's enduring: prayer remains a consistent spiritual habit.[19] Acts of service and volunteering still mark Christian engagement.[20] Practices like church attendance, Scripture reading, and giving have not disappeared[21] and are generally accepted as behavioral relevance in daily life.[22]

But how people practice their faith is evolving.

---

[19] *Religious Activity Increasing in the West,* Barna.com — Documents that prayer has remained consistently high over decades while other behaviors such as church attendance and volunteering have remained flat.

[20] *Beyond the Offering Plate: Views on Volunteering,* Barna.com — Reports that practicing Christians are significantly more likely than the general population to view regular volunteering and acts of service as important.

[21] *Young Adults Lead a Resurgence in Church Attendance,* Barna.com — Details trends in church attendance, including generational differences and overall patterns showing relative stability but not dramatic increases in traditional attendance frequency.

[22] Harvard T.H. Chan School of Public Health, "Religion and Health Study," ongoing: Research connects continued spiritual practices—including prayer and communal engagement—to psychological and social outcomes, indicating continued behavioral relevance.

Church attendance has become more sporadic, reflecting broader shifts in engagement and prioritization of faith in an individualized way.[23] Attendance patterns have changed among women, where they are declining.[24] Evangelism is increasingly questioned, especially among younger generations who often view it as relationally intrusive.[25] And while some of older generations are disengaging, Gen Z and Millennial men are showing renewed interest in gathering, mentoring, and sharing spiritual rhythms.[26] But traditional markers are being supplemented or replaced by more personal, flexible, and relational expressions of discipleship than churches are typically intentional with.[27]

If this changes nothing about what we do, we've missed it.

Practice hasn't declined, but it has decentralized.

---

[23] Barna Group, *"The Declining Importance of Faith: New Barna Findings,"* Barna.com

[24] Barna Group, *"New Research on Church Attendance: Decline of Women or the Rise of Men?"*

[25] *Younger Christians Say Evangelism Feels Coercive or Inappropriate*, Barna.com— Explores why Gen Z and Millennials increasingly view evangelism as offensive, pressuring, or culturally insensitive.

[26] *Young Adults Lead a Resurgence in Church Attendance, Barna.com* — Indicates that younger adults, particularly Gen Z and Millennials (including men), are attending church more frequently than older generations and that relational connection and mentoring opportunities outside of programming are key to sustaining this engagement.

[27] *Discipleship in Community, Barna.com* — Provides suggestions that relational expressions of discipleship are central to spiritual vibrancy.

Much of people practice their faith beyond church walls through conversations, households, friendships, and informal communities. This means if discipleship models are linear and church campus focused we may be missing potential influence.

People haven't stopped practicing their faith. They've stopped practicing it in predictable ways. Prayer endures. Service still inspires. But the where, when, and how of discipleship are no longer standardized or linear. It is often decoupled from the other dimensions.

Practically then, the metrics we use have to pivot.
We can no longer assume participation equals formation.
Nor can we assume absence equals apathy.

The question is not whether people are practicing faith. It's whether our structures still recognize where those practices are actually happening and whether we're willing to meet people there.

It's clear: avoid the necessary pivots, and the opportunity passes us by.

Affiliations: pursued, yet re-forming

Affiliation shows the same dynamics of enduring and yet also re-forming.

What's enduring: The physical church still matters. Many people continue to value the church as a place of community, spiritual safety, and formation.[28]

But the way people find affiliation is transforming.

Trust in church institutions is lower among younger adults and many question the church's authority or relevance to their lives.[29]

Most among younger generations seek communities that address real-world issues like mental health and social justice.[30] A significant portion of next-generation adults increasingly view the church as irrelevant to their lives.[31] It tends to be outside of

----

[28] *Five Trends Defining Americans' Relationship to Churches, Barna.com, —* Highlights how Americans continue to *maintain significant connection with church communities,* indicating that many still value the physical church as a place of community, meaning, and spiritual engagement even as familiar religious practices evolve.

[29] Barna Group, *Where Do Young Donors Place Trust? Barna.com* — Shows that trust in religious organizations and faith-based institutions varies by generation, with significant proportions of Gen Z and Millennials expressing reservations, including reluctance to trust churches with financial support—pointing to broader skepticism toward traditional institutional structures.

[30] Barna Group, *How Black Gen Z Understands Injustice and Church's Role, Barna.com, —* Shows that many Gen Z Christians view social concerns such as mental health, poverty, racial justice, and ending hunger and abuse as issues their faith and church involvement should address. Younger adults emphasize action on real-world issues alongside spiritual life.

[31] Barna Group, *What Young Adults Say Is Missing from Church, Barna.com, —* Reveals that many young adults (18–35) attending church identify aspects of worship and community that feel unfulfilled and report that church participation

the church walls, but many see value in online spaces while still desiring in-person connection.[32]

So, faith is obviously still present.
But like practices, affiliation is increasingly decentralized.[33]

When Data Feels Contradictory

We always want clean trends and predictable patterns.
But decoupling means little is linear.

Things move in tension.
Sometimes in paradox.
In overlapping realities that don't always resolve neatly.

You may have noticed this already:

A church being seen as valuable, while trust in it fades.
Commitment rising, while institutional connection declines.

---

often does not feel essential to their faith, signaling a level of disengagement from traditional church structures and expressions.

[32] Barna Group, *Christians Prefer In-Person Community for Church Activities, Barna.com,* — Finds that a significant majority of Christians believe that in-person experiences (community building, support, ministry to needs) are more meaningful than online alternatives, even while digital participation can supplement connection.

[33] Public Religion Research Institute, "The 2023 American Values Atlas": *Provides detailed state-by-state and generational affiliation patterns, showing both decline and persistence of religious belonging.*

Attendance is fluctuating, while relational engagement increases.
Respect for faith remaining, while beliefs diversify.

This is not to be taken as confusion.
It is more effective to see it as complexity.

Identity, beliefs, practices, and affiliations no longer align.
They move independently.
They accelerate at different speeds.
They sometimes collide in ways that seem inconsistent.

That's the result of decoupling.

The data can feel contradictory.
It isn't, really.
It simply reflects the complexity we're leading within.

You are not leading in a predictable environment anymore.
You are leading in a decentralized one.

And that changes how we lead.

We can no longer assume alignment.
We can no longer assume shared definitions.
We can no longer assume people move through faith in the same
order we did.

The old maps still exist.

They just don't describe the terrain anymore.

Moving Forward

So where do we go from here?

Let me frame four leadership pivots that will shape everything we discuss in the coming chapters.

First, embrace the complexity.
When churches treat Christians as a uniform audience, they oversimplify a landscape that is anything but simple. Faith formation no longer follows a single predictable path. It unfolds through different stories, different questions, and different starting points.

If we want to lead well, we must learn to see the room as it actually is. Our job isn't to manage the complexity, but to shepherd people through it and we will discuss how to do this while keeping our sanity.

Second, learn to read your context.
The research in this chapter shows what is happening across the board, but what is enduring and what is re-forming will look different in every community. Effective leadership now requires

contextual awareness. You cannot borrow someone else's assumptions. You must exegete your own environment.[34]

Third, lead with empathy, not just analysis.
This isn't merely an intellectual shift. It's a pastoral one.

People are navigating complexity in real time. They are sorting through identity, belief, practice, and belonging in ways that often feel disorienting to them.

We can't seek to eliminate that complexity.
We pastor people through it.

Fourth, think dimensionally.
Discipleship is no longer linear. Each dimension of faith develops differently and often asynchronously. People may belong before they believe. They may practice before they fully understand. They may identify long before they affiliate.

Spiritual growth now happens in seasons, not steps.

Another way to say it is this:

Faith has moved from the center of shared culture to the margins of personal life.

---

[34] See QR code for a practical guide on how to exegete your community.

It is still present. Still powerful.

But far more individualized and less institutional.

More personalized thus fragmented.

If we want to reach people, we must pivot toward them.

Not demand they pivot toward us.

We will talk about how to do this.

We can still build strong churches.

We can still form disciples.

We can still think in regard to scale.

But only if we restrain from trying to manage complexity and instead understand how to shepherd people through it.

To develop a strategy, preaching, or structure that does just that we have to make sure we think about change itself correctly.

That's where we turn next.

**Use the QR code to download the
free resources mentioned in this chapter.**

A Leadership Mindset For Change

No one puts new wine into old wine skins. Otherwise, the wine will burst the skins, and both the wine and the wineskins will be ruined. No, they pour new wine into new wineskins.

— Mark 2:22

The Leadership This Moment Requires - a preface

There's a temptation in leadership to rush from diagnosis to
solutions. But what if that instinct is exactly what this moment
punishes?

The more fragmented and splintered the world becomes, the
more fragile trust becomes. And when trust is fragile, leadership
cannot be built on certainty and formulas alone.

It must be built on something deeper.
Posture.

We have to start with ourselves before strategy. We have to talk
about the kind of leader this moment requires. Because methods
only work when the mindset beneath them can carry the weight
of change...

without becoming reactive or fearful.

Leadership requires a certain strain. As Paul writes in
Philippians 3:13–14, we must forget what's behind and press
forward toward what's ahead. Leading well means accepting the
discomfort of leaving the past and straining toward the future
God is calling us into.

To do this in a decoupled age, we need both empathy and clarity.

Clarity without empathy becomes cruelty.

Empathy without clarity becomes confusion.

This section is about becoming the kind of leader who can hold both in tension as you lead forward.

We cannot panic when the landscape shifts.

We must become more grounded as instability increases.

More attentive as complexity rises.

More curious when certainty feels out of reach.

More courageous when the pressure mounts.

Because let's be honest: the pressure pastors feel right now isn't just cultural.

It's personal.

You're not just leading through change.

You're leading through change while being criticized for it.

You're trying to mentor people who don't even agree on what words mean anymore.

You're trying to unify people who don't share the same information ecosystems.

You're trying to shepherd a community being discipled by a feed that reinforces whatever they already believe.

You're trying to make decisions with a lot of voices in your ear.

And if you aren't careful, you will start leading in ways that feel productive but are actually defensive:

Gripping tighter to your preference.
Simplifying too much.
Reacting abruptly to pushback.
Talking louder.
Assuming the worst in others.
Treating confusion like rebellion.
Treating questions like threats.

That posture may produce short-term control.
But it erodes long-term trust.

And in this environment, trust isn't a bonus.
It's the bridge.
It's the currency in an echo chamber world.

Without trust, you cannot correct.
You won't be able to issue a challenge.
You'll fail to bring your team to making decisions for change.
You cannot call people into maturity because they will not follow you there.

So before we rebuild anything outward, we must rebuild something inward.

The mindset for change within you and your team.

This section is about developing what I call a *Pivot Posture:*
a way of leading that doesn't deny disruption,
doesn't demonize the next generation,
doesn't romanticize the past,
and doesn't abandon conviction.

It's leadership with roots.
But leadership that can still pivot.

It means learning to lead without the crutch of predictability.
Learning to ask better questions.
Learning to listen without losing your spine.
Learning to stay emotionally present when you're frustrated.
Learning to shepherd people whose labels no longer tell you
what they believe or how they'll respond.

In other words, this section is about capacity.
The inner capacity of you and your team to be decisive and lead
forward in a fractured world.

Because the future of ministry will not belong to the loudest
church, the trendiest church,
or the most tech-savvy church.

It will belong to leaders who can
carry complexity without losing the gospel...
and without losing their soul.

4: Mission-Driven Empathy

People often ask me what I think about the "American church." My answer is always the same:

There's no such thing.

I obviously don't mean that churches don't exist in America. What I mean is that you can no longer talk about "the American church" as if it's a single, unified entity that you can describe and analyze. It's way too variegated. It's too diverse. It's too fragmented.

You might be able to talk about characteristics of the Western church versus the Eastern church in broad strokes. You might be able to identify some general trends. But "the American church" as a monolithic entity? That's not a thing. It's a thousand different things, each shaped by their own context, history, demographics, and theological commitments.

This matters because when we talk about church leadership we often assume a shared context that doesn't exist. We assume that what method works in one setting will work in another. We assume that churches face all the same challenges and can apply the same solutions.

The reality is far more complex. Which is why there is no one-size-fits-all model for ministry.

Of course there are similarities to what we face in ministry.

Of course there are things we will discuss regarding our leadership, preaching and discipleship. I'm going to help you see the patterns, pressures, and priorities that should shape how you lead in your setting.

But the main thing we must embrace is complexity.
And to do so with empathy.

The fragmentation shows up everywhere you look. A better understanding of the decoupling can help turn the network into a mosaic. It will help you see nuance, but get a picture. The key is to appropriately posture ourselves and our teams for change.

Leading Without A Shared Baseline

To understand why empathy is now mission-critical, you have to understand just how diverse the ministry landscape has become.

I'll start with denominations.

For most of American history, denominational identity carried real meaning. If someone told you they were Baptist, Methodist, Presbyterian, Lutheran, or Catholic, you had a fairly reliable sense of what they believed, how they practiced their faith, and where they found belonging. Denominational affiliation created a shared framework that made ministry more predictable.

That framework has been eroding for decades.

The rise of the non-denominational movement accelerated this shift. But "non-denominational" doesn't actually clarify much. It only tells you what a church isn't. It doesn't tell you what it believes, how it practices, or what theological instincts shape its culture. Two non-denominational churches can share almost nothing in common.

Even within historic denominations, diversity has exploded.[35] A Baptist church in one city may look nothing like a Baptist church in another. Some congregations maintain denominational ties but remove them from their public identity entirely. Labels that once provided clarity now often obscure more than they reveal.

---

[35] Association of Statisticians of American Religious Bodies, *2020 U.S. Religion Census: Religious Congregations & Membership in the United States* (Hartford, CT: U.S. Religion Census, 2023), — Reports that the number of participating religious bodies and congregations nationwide has grown substantially, with 372 religious bodies reporting over 350,000 congregations in 2020, compared with far fewer denominational bodies in earlier decades.

Then there is geographic diversity.

A church in rural Mississippi faces different realities than one in downtown Seattle. A congregation in suburban Dallas operates in a different cultural ecosystem than one in Brooklyn. Political assumptions, economic pressures, educational backgrounds, and social norms vary dramatically by region. Context shapes everything about how people hear and respond to the gospel.

Add generational complexity.

Many churches are now attempting to reach three or four generations at once. Yet, each is shaped by different cultural moments and different assumptions about truth, authority, and identity. Barna has described Gen Z as the "open generation." They are spiritually curious and willing to explore faith conversations. But they are not uniquely open to Christianity. They are open to everything. That openness creates both opportunity and instability.

Older generations carry different expectations about church, Scripture, authority, and belonging. These expectations don't always align. What feels obvious to one generation feels foreign to another.

And then there is theological diversity within a single congregation.

Within one church you may have:
Someone with a traditional view of Scripture
Someone reading it metaphorically
Someone unsure whether it holds authority at all

They may all call themselves Christians.
But what they mean by that word and how they live it can be
vastly different.

This is the new pastoral reality.

You are no longer leading a group of people who share the same
assumptions, vocabulary, or starting points. You are leading a
room filled with different stories, different frameworks, and
different expectations about what faith even means. Because,
that's the world we live in.

And all of that complexity lands on one group of people:

Pastors.

Diversity Can Create Pressure

I know firsthand how difficult this can be to navigate as a pastor.

During the height of the Black Lives Matter movement and
especially around the events surrounding George Floyd, leading
in Portland became extraordinarily complex. Within the same

congregation, I had some people insisting we place a BLM logo on our website or risk being labeled racist. At the very same time, others were telling me racism no longer existed.

Yes, you read that correctly and it was within the same church.

Portland is a unique context, and those were extreme positions. But the broader reality wasn't unique at all. The spectrum of conviction sitting in one congregation, and the pressure placed on leaders to validate one side or the other, is now common across the country.

You've likely felt this in your own context.

When cultural tensions rise, they don't stay outside the church. They walk through the front door and take a seat in the sanctuary. And both sides usually believe their view is not only correct, but morally necessary. Each expects the church and its leaders to affirm them.

That kind of pressure is immense.

Some leaders crumble under it.
Some fight back.
Some freeze.
Some absorb the anxiety of the system and thus amplify it.
Others learn to differentiate and lead with steadiness.

Navigating this level of complexity requires something deeper than strategy. It requires empathy. And not the soft, sentimental kind. The kind that allows you to see people clearly without being controlled by their reactions. The kind that allows you to remain present without becoming reactive.

Here's the point:

The diversity of today's cultural and theological landscape demands a new leadership posture.

Not one that gets tossed around by the loudest voices or latest controversies. Not one that retreats into defensiveness. But one that acknowledges how dramatically the landscape has changed and seeks to shepherd people wisely within it.

Pastoral leadership now requires what family systems theory calls a *non-anxious presence*: leaders who can remain grounded while others feel unsettled. Leaders who can hold conviction and compassion at the same time. Leaders who refuse to simplify people into categories and instead choose to shepherd them through complexity.

This is no longer optional.

The fragmented reality of the decoupled web means people process faith non-linearly and emotionally. They carry competing assumptions, conflicting information sources, and deeply personal convictions into the same community. Managing that complexity is not the goal.

Shepherding people through it is.

And that begins with mission-driven empathy.

Empathy As Starting Point

Thinking through our decoupled reality can make you want to throw your hands up and walk away.

I get it.

When everyone is processing faith differently...
when identity, belief, practice, and belonging no longer move together...
when labels don't tell you much anymore...
when every person seems to be operating from a different framework...

...it's easy to feel overwhelmed.

Where do you even begin?

The temptation can be to retreat into judgment. To look at the complexity and assume people are just confused, misled, or spiritually indifferent. To conclude that what they really need is to "get back to basics," pray more, just read their bible or return to the way things used to be.

But that posture won't serve the mission. And it won't serve the people we're called to shepherd either.

What if, instead of judging the complexity, we held it with empathy?

Empathy is not agreement.
It is not a theological compromise.
It is not lowering a standard of conviction.

Orthodox Christian truth still matters. What we believe about God, salvation, Scripture, and the person of Jesus matters enormously.

Empathy simply means doing the work to understand where people actually are...so we can lead them somewhere.

It means recognizing that decoupled processing is not something most people chose.

It's the sea they're swimming in.
It's the environment that shaped how they process everything.

Most people aren't intentionally fragmenting their faith. They're responding to a fragmented world.

Consider someone in their twenties who has grown up in an algorithm-shaped environment. From their earliest memories, information has been personalized, filtered, and curated. They've never lived in a world where everyone watched the same news, absorbed the same narratives, or shared the same cultural assumptions.

For them, a unified, integrated understanding of anything, including faith, is not normal. It's actually foreign.

And it feels isolating.

They've learned to process reality in fragments.
To pick what resonates.
To assemble meaning from pieces.

Is that confusing? Often.
Does it make discipleship harder? Absolutely.

But is it helpful to approach them with frustration for operating exactly the way their world trained them to operate?

No.

If we misdiagnose the environment as rebellion, we'll respond with correction when what's needed is shepherding. If we treat fragmentation as defiance, we'll speak louder when what's needed is deeper understanding.

Empathy is not sentimental.
It's strategic.

It allows us to see the person behind the posture.
The story behind the belief.
The questions beneath the resistance.

We don't start with fixing people.
We start with understanding them.

Because you can't disciple someone you haven't taken the time to see clearly.

And in a fragmented world, clarity begins with empathy.

From Assumption to Curiosity

Jesus never expected people to come to Him with a fully formed, integrated understanding of the Kingdom. He worked with what people brought. He met them where they were. Sometimes he asked questions. Sometimes he told stories that began with common experiences and led to unfamiliar conclusions.

But he always started where people actually were.

That is still the model.

Not judgment from a distance, but engagement up close.

Not waiting for people to sort themselves out, but walking with them as they process.

Not assuming understanding, but discovering it.

Which raises a practical challenge for us:

What do we do when we don't even know what someone means when they say they're a Christian?

That word used to signal something relatively clear: shared beliefs, shared practices, shared expectations. Now it tells you almost nothing beyond the fact that a conversation is beginning.

When someone tells me they're a Christian today, all I really know is that Jesus is somewhere in their vocabulary. I don't know what they believe about Scripture, salvation, morality, or authority. I don't know what practices shape their life. I don't know how they understand belonging or pursue it.

Labels no longer clarify.
They initiate discovery.

This requires a different leadership posture.

We can't assume.
We have to ask.
Then listen.

The pivot is simple but profound:

move from communicating first to curiosity first.

Not abandoning truth.
Not softening conviction.
But understanding before guiding.

Consider what happens when someone new walks into your church and says they're a Christian. What do you actually know about them?

Very little.

You don't know what they believe about God or Scripture.
You don't know their view of salvation or authority.
You don't know their past church experiences.
You don't know whether their faith is personal, cultural, or uncertain.
You don't know which dimension of faith (identity, belief, practice, or affiliation) is most alive for them right now.

All you know is they've used a familiar word with unfamiliar meaning.

This is why understanding the decoupled reality matters. It gives you a framework for discovery. A way to see what is actually shaping the person in front of you. A way to ask better questions and listen with greater clarity.

And yes, this can feel overwhelming.

If everyone is processing faith differently, how do you lead?
How do you disciple?
How do you scale anything?

Here's the hope: fragmentation is real, but it is not the end of the story.

When people are assembling faith from fragments, they are often more open than they appear. They are searching. They are trying to make sense of what they believe and why it matters. That openness creates opportunity for leaders who are willing to move toward people with humility and curiosity.

Recoupling rarely begins with you correcting.
It begins with understanding.

Before we try to align beliefs or shape practices, we must first learn how someone is actually processing faith. This is where the dimensional framework becomes a gift. It gives you language. It gives you clarity. It helps you and your team see what is really happening beneath the surface.

The question is whether we will be humble enough to lead this way.

Whether we will hold firmly to truth while holding loosely to our assumptions.

Whether we will choose curiosity over control.

Understanding over urgency.

Presence over pronouncement.

Humility. Curiosity. Adaptability.

These are not soft leadership traits. They are essential ones.

Because leading in this moment will require more than certainty.

It will require a change-ready posture capable of guiding your leaders through complexity without being threatened by it. When approached rightly, change does not threaten the mission.

It actually protects it. That can feel counterintuitive, but it's not. We'll talk about why next.

5: Change Protects Mission

Here's the thought we must always keep in front of us:
God's mission will always outlast the methods we love.

We often treat change like a threat to faithfulness. But the
opposite is usually true. The fact is, when we refuse to change,
we stop stewarding the mission.

Churches rarely drift off mission because culture shifts. They
drift because leaders confuse faithfulness to the mission
with faithfulness to familiar methods. But protecting the mission
has always required adaptation.

Always. Missing this point is a massive restraint to our mission.

History proves this again and again. And not just in a church
setting.

In 1865, as the Civil War was ending in the United States, a
mining engineer in southwestern Finland opened a small

wood-pulp mill near the Tammerkoski Rapids. Six years later, he opened another mill along the Nokianvirta River. That second location eventually inspired the name of a company that would become one of the most adaptive organizations of the modern era:

Nokia.

Over the next century, Nokia repeatedly reinvented itself.
From wood pulp to rubber.
From rubber to cables.
From cables to electronics.
From electronics to mobile phones.

Each pivot strengthened the company rather than weakening it.
Why? Because they understood something essential:
their mission of "connecting people" mattered more than their methods or the product they offered.

As the world changed, they adapted how they fulfilled that mission. And for decades, it worked.

From 1979 through the early 2000s, Nokia dominated the mobile phone industry. They introduced the first car phone, one of the first handheld mobile phones, and eventually sold their billionth device. It seemed like they couldn't miss.

But within a few short years, everything changed.

Smartphones reshaped the market. Competitors adapted quickly.

Nokia didn't.

In 2011, their CEO famously told employees they were standing on a "burning platform." The company that had mastered adaptation for over a century suddenly couldn't pivot fast enough to keep up with the moment.

What happened?

They settled into what had once worked. They clung to comfortable methods even as the world shifted beneath them. And, when they got comfortable in the status quo, they were left behind.

It happens all the time, but it doesn't have to be your story.

Consistency is important for any organization, but it's also true that organizations don't usually collapse because they change too much. They collapse because they stop changing when the mission requires it.

Change Is Not An Enemy

We resist change because we think we're protecting what matters most. We can even define success as staying the same.

But often, the opposite is true.

In a changing world, the only way to protect the mission
is to change our methods of operation. Not for the sake of
change, of course. It's for the sake of the mission.

Yet many leaders treat change like an adversary. Something to
fight. Something to avoid. Something that threatens faithfulness.

There is comfort in doing things the way we always have.
Familiar methods feel safe. Predictable. Proven. They become
intertwined with our identity.

But we no longer live in a predictable world.

We live in an era where change is not optional.
It is required for survival, growth, and mission.

Organizations that refuse to change eventually die.
Not because their mission failed, but because their methods did.

The thing to remember is: **When you grip a method too tightly,
you eventually choke the mission.**

The moment you protect methods over a mission, you quietly put
a timestamp on your future. Our methods serve the mission.
Well...until they don't. This is how the world has always worked.

Communities change.

Demographics shift.

Technology reshapes attention.

Language evolves.

Assumptions disappear.

Information is obtained in new ways.

When these things change, leaders must change how they lead.
Not because the truth has changed, but because people have.

One of the most dangerous assumptions in ministry is this:
If we change our methods, we are compromising our
faithfulness.

But faithfulness to the mission has always required adaptation.

God's mission has not changed.
Reaching people with the gospel is still the goal.
Forming disciples is still the calling.
Seeing lives transformed is still the hope.

What must change is how we pursue that mission in a changing
world.

This is where many leaders get stuck. We treat common
approaches as if they were sacred. We assume that changing how
we do something means changing what we believe.

But methods are not doctrine.
And tradition is not the same as truth.

Holding firmly to truth while loosening our grip on methods is
not a compromise. It is stewardship.

Change is not the enemy of the church.
Misplaced loyalty to our methods is.

Missionaries Contextualize

My friend Mark Strong has pastored in Portland, Oregon, for
more than 35 years. He planted a church in a particular
neighborhood with a simple mission: reach people where they
are physically, emotionally and spiritually.

And now for over three decades, that church has remained a
pillar in its community.

But not because the neighborhood stayed the same.
It didn't at all.

Portland has become one of the most rapidly gentrified cities in
the country. Entire neighborhoods have shifted economically,
culturally, and demographically. Long-time residents moved out.
New residents moved in. The community Mark originally
planted in looks very different today.

Yet the church still stands. Still reaching people. Still transforming lives. Why?

Because Mark never confused his methods with his mission.

His convictions stayed the same. His commitment to the gospel never shifted. Thus his methods adapted as his community changed.

Reaching the neighborhood always mattered more than preserving his preferences. The mission always mattered more than familiarity.

That's what missionaries do.
They contextualize.

They learn the language of the people they're sent to reach. They understand the culture. They adjust their approach so the message can actually be heard.

Not because the message changes, but because people do.

When I planted a church in Portland, I had almost no connections. I parachuted into a city where I knew almost no one and started from scratch. Everything about how we did church had to be shaped by the specific context we were trying to reach.

Portland loves small and local. Quaint. Independent. Neighborhood-driven.

So we structured our church to reflect that reality. We built around geographic communities and local schools. I often described our approach as "growing by staying smaller." That wasn't driven primarily by theology. It was driven by context. We were trying to remove unnecessary barriers so people could actually engage.

What worked in Portland wouldn't necessarily work somewhere else. Because contextualization is always local. But the principle is universal:

The mission stays the same. The methods must therefore adapt.

Missionaries have always understood this.
Church leaders sometimes forget it.

We can hold tightly to truth while holding loosely to methods. Otherwise, maintaining methods becomes the mission. It might be unintentional. But it's inevitable.

Change Protects Mission

So, we continue to ask the questions: What if change isn't a threat to your mission—but a protector of it?

What if adapting isn't a strategic option but a spiritual responsibility?

Every organization eventually faces this tension. What once worked begins to lose effectiveness. Methods that once carried the mission start to slow it down. And leaders must decide whether they are more committed to advancing purpose over everything else.

Organizations are living systems.
They either adapt or they decline.

When leaders hold too tightly to "the way it's always been," they often believe they are protecting what matters most. In reality, they may be protecting methods that no longer serve the mission.

But when you begin to see change as a means of protecting the mission, everything shifts.

You move from:
defensive to intentional,
reactive to proactive,
fearful to faithful.

Change becomes an ally instead of an adversary.
A vehicle instead of a threat.

And when leaders frame change this way, people rally.
Resistance softens.
Energy returns.

One of the most important mindset shifts you can make as a leader is this:

Change is not the enemy of mission.
Refusing to change is.

We cannot seek the transformation of people and communities without the ability to change ourselves. The methods that once served your mission well will not serve it forever. Communities shift. People change. Culture moves.

The good news is God's mission will outlive the methods we love. So, if the mission matters most, then adapting our methods isn't a compromise. It's stewardship.

Leaders Go First

This is where it becomes personal.

Most of us entered ministry because we want to see change.
Changed hearts.
Changed lives.
Changed communities.

Yet it's strangely easy for leaders who call others to transformation to resist it themselves.

We preach repentance. We teach growth. We call people forward.

But when change confronts our own systems, preferences, or leadership habits, we hesitate.

If we want to lead people through change, we have to go first.

Your adaptability becomes permission for others. Your humility becomes an invitation. Your willingness to adjust becomes proof that change is not something to fear.

Again, here's the truth: The methods that served your mission in one season will not necessarily serve it in the next.

That isn't failure. That's leadership. Your own openness to change is the entry for the adaptability of your team.

Healthy leaders regularly evaluate their methods and ask:
Is this still helping us accomplish our mission?
Or has it quietly become the mission itself?

Systems naturally try to preserve themselves. Leaders must ensure they still serve the mission. If we become more committed to our methods than our mission, we will defend what eventually no longer works.

If we stay committed to the mission, we will adapt whenever necessary to advance it. This mindset is the first step. But sustaining it requires something deeper than strategy.

It requires leaders who begin by examining themselves.

Because the greatest barrier to change is rarely external. It's internal.

6: Barriers To Change

Every leader says they want change.

Fewer leaders are willing to lead it.

Not because they lack vision.
Not because they don't understand what needs to happen.
But because the real barriers to change are rarely strategic.

They're personal.

If you are responsible for leading an organization, then leading change is not optional. It is part of stewarding the mission you've been entrusted with. But it is also deeply personal work. Because every change you lead will surface fears, in others and in yourself.

So it starts with you.

You must model the mindset that change is not just a requirement for sustaining a mission, but a privilege. A privilege because you are shaping the future of the people and the organization you lead.

When leaders treat change as a tool for protecting mission while honoring the past, something powerful happens. Trust grows. Alignment forms. Movement begins.

Change stops feeling like disruption and starts feeling like stewardship.

But even leaders who believe this get stuck.

I've seen it in others.
I've seen it in myself.

Which is why we have to be honest about what actually blocks change.

Where Change Gets Stuck

Most barriers to change live inside the leader before they ever show up inside the organization.

Yes, there are structural challenges: budgets, systems, stakeholders, programs, history.

But underneath almost every structural barrier is a relational and emotional one.

Change affects people. People have histories.
And those histories are woven into ministries.

And relationships.

This is why change in a ministry context can feel especially complex. You're not just adjusting strategy. You're disrupting relational ecosystems. People who have served faithfully for years suddenly feel uncertain about their place. Roles shift. Rhythms change. Long-standing relationships get reconfigured.

If leaders fail to recognize the relational weight of change, resistance will feel confusing and frustrating. But it isn't confusing at all.

Change threatens: identity, competence, belonging, security.

When those feel at risk, people instinctively move into self-protection.

That's when resistance shows up.
That's when teams stall.
That's when leaders quietly avoid the very changes they know are necessary.

So before we talk about personal barriers inside you, we need to address how to lead people through the relational dynamics of change well.

There are four reframes that help leaders move an organization from defensive to being change-ready.

Four Ways of Reducing Resistance to Change

1. Acknowledge and articulate the fear

Change activates basic human fears:
loss,
irrelevance,
failure,
uncertainty.

If you don't name those realities, they will quietly control the room.

Most leadership cultures avoid emotional language. But ignoring fear doesn't eliminate it. It amplifies it. When leaders acknowledge what people may be feeling, it lowers defensiveness and creates space for healthy processing.

You are not validating resistance.
You are making it discussable.

I've missed this at times in my own leadership.
It always made change harder.

2. Inspire a growth mindset

People with a fixed mindset experience change as threat:
Will I still matter?
Will I still be good at my role?
Will I be replaced?

A growth mindset reframes change as development:
What can I learn?
How can I grow?
Where is this taking us?

Leaders set this tone. When you consistently connect change to growth people begin to see possibility instead of loss. You do this both for the organization's growth and for the individuals involved.

3. Clearly link every change to mission

Nothing reduces resistance like clarity of purpose.

When people only hear what is changing, they resist.
When they understand why it matters to the mission, they are much more likely to engage.

Never assume the connection is obvious.
Say it repeatedly.

Help people see how the change protects what matters most.
Fear turns into action when purpose becomes clear.

4. Differentiate vision from ideas

In seasons of change, loose ideas create chaos and anxiety.

Teams don't need more brainstorming.
They need clarity.

Ideas are possibilities you're processing. Vision gives clear
direction:
What we are doing.
Why?
When.
How it will work.
Where people fit.

Ambiguity fuels resistance. Clarity reduces it.

If you are a verbal processor, be careful. Make sure you always
preface brainstorm so your team doesn't take it as direction.
Leaders often miss this. Your voice as the leader carries weight
so your team will take what you say seriously. In times of change
clarity is a must, so be sure to clarify ideas versus vision.

That said …

Even when you lead change well organizationally, something else
still stands in the way.

The most stubborn barriers are not in your systems.
They're less about the words you choose.
They are more about the internal tensions alive inside you.

Internal Barriers

Organizational barriers to change are real. But the deepest
barriers are personal. They live inside the leader.

Every change carries relational risk for a leader. Approval is
threatened. Relationships shift. Expectations collide. And if
those dynamics go unexamined, leaders stall. Not because they
don't know what to do, but because they feel the cost of doing it.

**Change won't move through your team
until it moves through you.**

Leaders don't push change.
They model it.

And every leader is influenced by four "teams." You may not
consciously name them, but they shape your decisions, your
courage, and your hesitation.

These teams will either free you to lead change...
or quietly barricade you from it.

Team #1: Who You Work For

Every leader answers to someone.

Yes, ultimately to the Lord.
Yes, structurally maybe to a board.

But in the moment of decision, there is almost always a specific person whose approval weighs most.

An elder.
A donor.
A spouse.
A predecessor.
A staff member.
An influential family.

You're considering a change... and your mind goes straight to them:

What will they think?
How will this affect our relationship?
Will they support me or resist me?
Who else will their opinion influence?

If you're not careful, that person is functionally who you're working for at that moment.

And if fear of their reaction keeps you from acting, you've identified your barrier.

I've watched leaders stall for years because of one influential voice. I've seen them freeze because they couldn't bear disappointing a mentor. I've seen organizations stay stuck because peace with a few people mattered more than progress for the mission.

Those relationships matter.

But when preserving approval outweighs stewarding mission, leadership stops.

You must learn to name who you're working for in each decision and decide whether their approval should carry that much weight. This isn't easy. There is always a cost. But working for the wrong person has a much higher price.

Team #2: Who You're Working With

These are your closest ministry partners.
Staff. Elders. Key leaders.

When aligned, they accelerate change.
You dream together. Challenge each other. Carry the mission together.

When misaligned, they become the greatest barrier.

Every change becomes a negotiation.
Energy shifts from mission to internal management.
Momentum slows.

This is where many leaders quietly compromise.

They keep people in key roles who no longer share the future because:

they've been around a long time,
they're loved,
they hold relational capital.

But you cannot take people into the future if they're committed to preserving the past. It's possible to have the right person but in the wrong position. Alignment on mission is not negotiable, regardless of how much someone might be beloved.

Healthy teams allow disagreement.
But they require alignment.

Without shared commitment to mission and direction, change becomes nearly impossible.

And sometimes the most loving leadership decision is acknowledging misalignment instead of pretending it will turn into momentum.

Team #3: Who's Working For You

These are the people who execute the ministry daily.

Staff. Ministry leads. Volunteers.

For change to move, you need people who are:
teachable,
adaptable,
mission-driven.

Not just loyal to the past.

If this group resists change, everything slows: hesitation, second-guessing, passive resistance, gossip, loss of energy.

And if you tolerate misalignment here, the organization eventually follows their pace, not yours.

Hiring is a mission strategy.
So is releasing people.

When leaders avoid hard staffing decisions, they unintentionally choose stagnation.

You are not just preserving relationships. Unfortunately, you are allowing resistance to shape the future.

And the real question underneath those decisions is often:

Who am I trying to please?
And what is that costing the mission?

Team #4: Who's Working On You

This may be the most important team of all.

Mentors. Coaches. Advisors. Counselors.
People outside your system who can see you clearly.

Senior leaders especially need this. Inside your organization, everyone is affected by your decisions. That means feedback is often filtered. Intentionally or not it is nearly impossible for someone within your organization to give truly unbiased feedback.

So, without outside voices:
pressure becomes guidance,
noise becomes wisdom,
stress becomes direction.

Leaders without this team tend to react to whoever is loudest, closest, or hardest to disappoint.

But when people are working on you:
you gain perspective,
you see patterns,
you process before reacting,
you lead instead of absorbing pressure.

If no one is working on you, you will eventually be worked by pressure.

Pressure doesn't propel the mission. It pulls leaders into self-preservation, where energy is guarded, tension is avoided, and survival quietly replaces calling.

Why This Matters

I often refer to these four teams as the *bookends principle*.

Teams one and four hold everything else up.

If you don't know whose approval is shaping your decisions you won't lead with clarity. And if you don't have people working on you, you won't see clearly enough to lead change.

Those two realities stabilize everything else.

Because these four teams shape every leadership decision you make. They influence your courage, your hesitation, your clarity, your compromise.

When they're strong you can align the people you work with, you can lead the people who report to you, you can make decisions rooted in mission, not pressure.

But when either bookend is missing, the system begins to tilt.

You'll start leading from approval-seeking instead of conviction.
You'll react instead of discern.
You'll feel stuck without knowing why.

And the people around you will feel it, even if they can't name it.

So before you think about changing systems, strategies, or structures...start here.

Ask yourself:

Who am I really working for in this decision?
Who am I working with and are we aligned?
Who is working for me and are they adaptable?
And who is working on me, helping me see clearly?

Because the barriers to change are personal before they're organizational.

When those barriers remain hidden, change stalls.
When they're named, movement becomes possible.

And this is where leadership pivots.

From managing systems...
toward stewarding the mission.

Once that shift happens, change stops feeling like disruption and starts becoming responsibility.

Which means the real work ahead isn't just organizational.

It has a lot to do with you, personally.

7: Moving the Needle

Everyone talks about moving the needle.

We want progress.
We want growth.
We want impact.
We want things to change for the better.

But here's what actually moves the needle:

Decisions.

Not conversations about decisions.
Not planning for decisions.
Not hoping things will improve.
Not more ideas about what could be.

Decisions.

Actual choices that commit resources, set direction, and move an organization from where it is to where it must go.

Yet, the Church has a paralysis problem.

If we sense a need for change...
We form committees.
We conduct studies.
We gather input.
We process options.

But too often, we never decide.

And I understand why. Decisions are costly.
They eliminate other options.
They create consequences.
They invite criticism.
They force people to adjust.
They put leadership on the line.

So we wait.
We discuss and hope for clarity that feels safe.

But here's the truth: **Indecision is not neutral.** It is a decision.

When you don't decide, you're deciding to stay where you are.
You're deciding the status quo is safer than movement. You're

deciding that fear of being wrong outweighs the cost of doing nothing.

And over time, that decision compounds.

Because while you delay, the culture keeps moving. Your people keep changing. Your mission keeps drifting out of alignment with your methods.

So, here's what every leader must eventually accept:

No decision is almost always the worst decision.

Paralysis never advances a mission. It only allows slow drift while leaders wait for certainty that rarely comes.

And the mission is too important to allow drift that should be avoided.

A Relational Reality

There is a good reason many ministry leaders struggle with decision-making.

Pastoral leadership is relational at its core.

Shepherds are wired to care for people where they are. We think about the flock. 1 Peter 5:2 comes to mind.

We consider how decisions affect individuals.
We carry names and stories, not just strategies and systems.

This is a beautiful quality. The church should be relationally centered. We are not a corporation optimizing for profit. We are a community being formed by the Spirit.

But this relational strength has a shadow side.

When it comes to decisions, relational leaders can drift into people-pleasing. Protecting relational peace rather than the mission. And this quietly robs us of missional leadership.

Here's how it plays out.

You're considering a change that would serve the mission. But instead of starting with the mission, your mind goes to individuals:

Betty will be upset.
Joe will push back.
That family might leave.
A key volunteer may step away.

Before you've made a decision, you're already carrying the emotional weight of everyone's potential response.

Sound familiar?

When leaders begin by calculating reactions, decisions stall.
The social system feels heavy and it weighs down
decision-making.

Every possible response becomes another reason to delay. And
slowly, the mission takes a back seat to managing perceptions.

This is the "who are you working for?" barrier we discussed
earlier. If you aren't careful, the loudest or most influential voices
begin shaping decisions before they're even made.

Here's the pivot to consider:

Decide for the mission first.
Shepherd people through the decision second.

This isn't about ignoring people.
It's about sequencing.

First ask:
What best serves our mission?
What decision aligns with our calling?
What is most faithful in the long run?

Make that decision.

Then begin the pastoral work:
communicating clearly,

listening carefully,

walking patiently with people as they process.

Shepherding is still essential.
It just comes after clarity, not before it.

I think of Moses in the desert. Can you imagine him trying to solve everyone's tensions before moving forward? Staying stuck would've been the only choice. Because, when you try to shepherd every reaction before deciding, you'll rarely decide at all. But when you decide with the mission in view, you can shepherd with honesty and confidence.

You are not called to keep everyone comfortable.
You are called to lead God's people toward God's mission.

And that requires decisions.

The Paralysis of Indecision

In 1975, a Kodak engineer named Steve Sasson invented the first digital camera. It worked. It captured images. And it had the potential to make Kodak's film business obsolete.

When executives saw it, their response was essentially: "That's interesting... but don't tell anyone." This is classic. The comfort of their current success caused them to lose sight of what was best for the long-term mission of the company.

For the next two decades, Kodak wrestled with a decision: Should they protect their film business or embrace the digital future they had just invented?

Eventually they commissioned a major research study to answer the question: Would digital photography actually replace film?

The results were clear: Digital photography would eventually dominate. But Kodak had time, roughly ten years, to prepare and pivot.

Ten years.

They had invented the technology. They had the research. They had the head start.

What they didn't have was decisive leadership.

Kodak hesitated. They experimented without committing. They innovated without strategically pivoting. And their indecision cost them everything. They didn't lose out on being the dominant force in digital photography because they made one bad decision.

They lost because they delayed the necessary one. To pivot.

Today Kodak still exists in different industries, but its dominance in photography is gone.

Not because they lacked insight.

Because they lacked resolve.

Indecision is one of the greatest enemies of progress.

When leaders hesitate too long, the entire organization feels it.

Energy stalls.

Momentum fades.

Confidence erodes.

And culture always mirrors the uncertainty of leadership.

Ministries are not immune to this. In fact, they are more susceptible to this cultural decay.

When leaders delay necessary decisions — about structure, staffing, strategy, or direction — the organization slowly drifts into paralysis. Conversations multiply. Committees form. Opinions circulate. But forward movement stops.

And here's the irony:

No single wrong decision is as costly as chronic indecision.

A wrong decision can be corrected.

A wrong decision can teach.

A wrong decision can even build trust when owned quickly.

That means, the decision isn't actually "wrong."
But indecision drains momentum.
It confuses teams.
It quietly communicates that clarity isn't coming.

Healthy organizations learn through action.
They decide, evaluate, adjust, and keep moving. That's the formula.

This is the leadership pivot to consider:

Don't obsess over making the perfect decision. Make the best decision you can, then work to make it be the right one.

Movement creates learning.
Learning creates clarity.
Clarity builds momentum.

Indecision does the opposite.
It makes pivoting nearly impossible because nothing ever actually moves.

Inaction breeds frustration.
Even imperfect direction breeds purpose.

Every meaningful decision carries risk.
Every change introduces uncertainty.

But leaders who protect the mission don't wait for certainty. They move forward with conviction, humility, and the willingness to adjust along the way.

Because the mission doesn't stall from making the wrong decision. It stalls when leaders refuse to make one at all.

Decision and Shepherding

The early church did not treat decision-making as optional. It treated it as essential to protecting the mission.

Scripture shows a pattern: apostles and shepherds working together. Different roles, different instincts, one mission.

They thought differently.
They moved at different speeds.
They carried different burdens.

And that tension was intentional.

In Acts, when major issues threatened the unity and direction of the church, leaders didn't avoid decisions. They made them. The debate over circumcision is a clear example. Local communities wrestled with the issue, but the apostles stepped in to discern, decide, and clarify what would protect the mission moving forward.

They had a wider vantage point. They weren't embedded in the relational pressures of a single congregation. They could see the implications for the whole movement.

Then local shepherds implemented those decisions, walking people through the change relationally and pastorally.

That pattern matters and why I emphasize the sequencing of making decisions for the mission first, then shepherding second.

The church needs leaders who think organizationally and leaders who shepherd relationally. Both are gifts. Both are necessary. Ephesians 4 reminds us that different leadership functions exist to build and mature the body together. The gifts bring about different ways of seeing people and ministry. This is by design.[36]

If you only have organizational thinkers, decisions get made that ignore people and leave relational damage behind.

If you only have relational thinkers, decisions often never get made and the mission slowly stalls.

Which means this is not an either/or conversation.
It's a both/and design.

---

[36] See the QR code at the end of this chapter for a chart that breaks down how each gift in this passage practically manifests in leadership.

Most ministry teams naturally lean relational. That's who ministry attracts — shepherds, caregivers, people who feel the weight of individuals deeply. That is a strength.

But it also creates a vulnerability.

Without intentional space for organizational clarity, relational leaders can feel every potential objection before the decision is made.

Paralysis follows.

This is why you must learn to rise above the relational weight long enough to ask:

What serves the mission best?

Make that decision.

Then return to the relational work of shepherding people through it.

That sequence protects both the mission and the people.

On the other hand, some leaders carry a more apostolic orientation. They naturally think about those not yet reached, the city beyond the church walls, the future more than the present.

This is also a gift.
But it too carries its own risk.

Leaders who always look ahead can unintentionally move too
fast, leaving people behind, creating exhaustion and instability
inside the community they're trying to lead forward.

Which means they must learn to listen to shepherding voices.
Those who help discern timing, pace, and care.

Healthy leadership requires both instincts.
Decision and shepherding.
Clarity and compassion.
Movement and care.

The mission advances when these work together.

And here's the point for this chapter:
Decisions are not unspiritual. They are part of how God leads
His people forward.

The apostles decided.
The shepherds walked with people through those decisions.
And the Church moved.
Of course there was tension.
But the mission moved forward with clarity.

It still works the same way.

Making A Call

You can never eliminate all risk in a decision.
You will never have perfect information.
At some point, you just have to make the call.

Many church leaders feel pressure to ensure everyone is fully on board before moving forward. That sounds caring. Sometimes it is. But in seasons of change, it can also become a trap.

Overthinking is often just fear wearing a thinking cap.
Overanalyzing turns crossroads into parking lots.
And parking lots are full of cars that stand still.

Stagnation should never be confused with faithfulness.

Here's the truth:
The needle only moves when decisions are made.

Every organization eventually gets stuck when leaders hesitate to decide. When that happens, meetings multiply, tension grows, and momentum slowly dies.

One reason this happens is because leaders confuse collaboration with consensus.

This distinction is crucial.

Collaboration means you gather the right people, listen well, invite honest input, and consider different perspectives. Then the leader makes a decision and owns it. Collaboration values voices, but it doesn't require total agreement. The leader takes on the accountability for the decision.

Consensus means you wait until everyone is comfortable. And that almost always leads to delay, compromise, and diluted outcomes. Unanimous agreement is rare, especially when decisions actually matter. When consensus becomes the goal, the most hesitant voices end up controlling direction.

That's how teams drift into discussion without decision. That's also how indecisive leaders hide. They use the team's "process" to hide their own fear of making the wrong decision.

But: discussion without decision is just the illusion of progress.

Meetings become roundabouts: lots of motion, no clear direction. Over time, energy fades. Emotional capacity drops. Teams slip into maintenance mode and keep circling. People stop expecting change and start protecting what is.

You've probably seen it happen.

In a consensus-driven meeting, conversation slowly shifts toward keeping everyone comfortable. Strong personalities dominate. Quieter voices withdraw. The meeting grows longer, the plan grows weaker, and the outcome is predictable:

"Let's revisit this next week."

Nothing moves.
No one is sent.
Little if anything to do.
The mission stalls.

In a collaborative environment, something different happens. The leader listens carefully. Draws out quieter voices. Considers the gathered input. But eventually, the leader decides and then explains why, clarifies direction, assigns next steps, and moves forward.

Not everyone has to agree. It can just be a step forward. A direction. But everyone knows their role.

That's the difference:

Collaboration invites input.
Consensus requires permission.

Collaboration honors people.
Consensus surrenders leadership.

And surrendered leadership always leads to a stalled mission — even when it's framed as being a team effort. A team isn't an option. No one person can claim victory. But one leader can use

the idea of working as a team to hide their inability to make a
decision.

Pivoting in this moment will require courage.
You will not have perfect conditions.
You will not have complete agreement.
You will be misunderstood by some and criticized by others.

But an imperfect decision made with humility and adjusted
along the way is far less damaging than refusing to decide at all.

So make the call.
Move forward.
Shepherd people through it the best you can.
Adjust as needed.

Because paralysis protects nothing and costs you everything.

**Use the QR code to download the
free resources mentioned in this chapter.**

8: The Can-If Mentality

Every organization has a list of reasons why it can't change.

We can't because we don't have the budget.
We can't because the building won't accommodate it.
We can't because the staff is stretched too thin.
We can't because the congregation won't understand.
We can't because the board won't approve it.
We tried something like that before and it didn't work.
Yeah, but that's not how we do things here.

The list is endless.

And here's the difficult truth: every line on the can't-because list usually carries some truth. Constraints are real. Budgets are finite. Buildings have limits. Staff get tired. History matters. Relationships matter. All of it matters.

But here's the mindset pivot that separates organizations that move forward from those that stagnate:

Every "can't because" can be reframed as a "can if."

We can if we adjust the budget.

We can if we rethink how we use the building.

We can if we shift staff priorities.

We can if we communicate more clearly.

We can if we learn from what didn't work last time.

We can if we cast vision to the board.

We can if we challenge how we've always done things.

Same obstacles.

Same tensions.

Completely different posture.

"Can't because" treats every challenge like a wall.

"Can if" treats every challenge like a tension to navigate.

That difference determines whether an organization stalls or moves in a direction.

This isn't just semantics.

Language shapes thinking.

Thinking shapes culture.

And culture determines whether a mission advances or drifts.

When leaders consistently operate from a can't-because posture, teams become defensive and cautious. Energy drops. Creativity shrinks. Meetings become problem-naming sessions instead of problem-solving sessions. Blameshifting becomes the core form of communication.

But when leaders adopt a can-if posture, the same obstacles become invitations to adapt. Energy rises. Collaboration increases. Solutions begin to surface.

This is one of the simplest leadership shifts you can make. And one of the most powerful.

A Story of Can-If Thinking

In 1981, a retail executive named Howard Schultz visited a small coffee-bean shop in Seattle called Starbucks. He was struck by the aroma, the passion, and the potential.

After joining the company, Schultz traveled to Europe and encountered espresso cafés that functioned as community hubs. He saw places where people gathered, lingered, worked, and talked. He returned convinced that Starbucks could become something more than a store selling coffee beans.

We can transform how America experiences coffee.
We can create spaces where people gather.
We can build a third place between home and work.

But Starbucks leadership couldn't see it.

We can't because that's not our model.

We can't because it's too risky.

We can't because we don't know that business.

We can't because people won't sit and drink coffee.

So Schultz left. He started his own coffee company built on a different mindset:

We can if we build the model.

We can if we learn how to sustain it.

We can if we create spaces people actually want to be.

Two years later, he bought Starbucks and led its expansion into what it is today.

A can-if mindset didn't ignore reality.

It looked at possibility.

It named the obstacles and then built a path through them.

Every organization has moments like this.

Moments where the future is sitting just beyond current assumptions.

Moments where the difference between stagnation and movement is simply how leaders interpret the tension lying before them.

The Can't-Because Trap

Every leader has experienced the meeting where a new idea surfaces and the room instantly shifts into defensive mode:

"We can't afford that."
"We can't do that with our staffing."
"Our people won't want that."
"We're too busy."

Once you start noticing this mindset, you'll see it everywhere.

The problem with can't-because thinking isn't that it names constraints. It's that it treats them as final.

It closes the door on possibility.
It halts momentum.
It suffocates innovation.
It reinforces a fixed mindset that slowly protects the very stagnation leaders say they want to avoid.

Your mission doesn't die when culture shifts.
Your mission dies when decision-making freezes.

A can-if mindset doesn't pretend obstacles aren't real.

It simply refuses to let them be the final word.

Shifting to "Can If"

A pivot-ready leader recognizes that tension is normal. Obstacles are normal. Challenges are normal. The question is not whether they exist, but how we interpret them and how we engage them.

A can-if mindset does at least four powerful things.

1. It Builds Up the Team

When everyone is working to solve a problem instead of defending a limitation, collaboration increases. The team becomes energized. New voices emerge. The problem becomes shared rather than assigned.

2. It Treats Tension as Opportunity

Tension isn't a stop sign. It's a signal. It tells you where innovation is needed. Can-if thinking reframes tension as the birthplace of progress. Can't-because thinking turns specific situations into systemic problems. Can-if thinking treats every situation as a choice of tensions rather than a closed door.

3. It Accelerates Creativity

When you ask, "How could this work?" instead of "Why won't this work?" the brain shifts into generative mode. This is where imagination and new solutions come from. Possibilities surface that would otherwise stay buried.

4. It Increases Momentum

Teams move faster when they're focused on what's possible. Enthusiasm rises. Engagement grows. People lean in with energy instead of checking out or staying dormant. The ceiling for higher capacity leaders rises so they stay on the team longer.

And here's the bonus: the can-if mindset benefits the leader too.

Leaders become more trusted because people see them pursuing possibility instead of policing limitations. Leaders solve problems proactively. Leaders stay ahead of challenges rather than reacting to crises. Leaders empower teams to find solutions instead of bottlenecking every decision.

Organizations benefit as well — faster decision-making, higher resilience, greater innovation, and stronger adaptability all become part of the culture.

Can-if doesn't just change language. It changes culture. And culture determines whether the mission stays the priority.

Where to Begin

If this feels far from your current reality, that's okay. It's more normal than you might think.

Shifting from can't-because to can-if is a cultural transformation, not a slogan. But you can begin leading your team toward this more creative and proactive posture with a few simple practices.

1. Lead with Questions
Ask: What needs to be true to make this work?
What opportunities exist inside this challenge?

Questions move people out of defensiveness and into discovery.

2. Reframe Every Can't-Because Statement
When someone says, "We can't because...," respond with:
"Let's reframe that. We can do this if what takes place?"

Over time this becomes the natural language of the team.

3. Celebrate Innovation Publicly
If you want more creativity, reward it. Celebrate attempts and effort, not just outcomes. Show that experimenting is safe so anxiety around failure is suppressed. When people fear failure, creativity dies quickly.

4. Create a Safe Environment for Risk
A can-if culture embraces calculated risk. Failure becomes feedback, not condemnation. How you respond to risk-taking will determine whether innovation grows or disappears.

This mindset shift is learned behavior.

It won't happen overnight.

But with consistency, it becomes the dominant culture of the organization and a powerful engine for change.

A Final Starbucks Lesson

When Schultz returned to Starbucks in 2008, he wasn't done with can-if thinking. He led a reinvention around technology and it was a risky move at the time. But he saw possibilities where others saw barriers. The Starbucks app became one of the most widely used rewards platforms in the world.

It reminds me of something often attributed to Henry Ford. When asked why he pursued innovation beyond what customers requested, he said that if he had simply asked people what they wanted, they would have asked for a faster horse.

That's the power of can-if thinking.

You discover potential where others see limits.

You find openings where others see obstacles.

You build the future instead of defending the past.

Healthy and growing organizations make this shift.

Stagnant ones rarely do.

So what's on your can't-because list?

What obstacles have you accepted as final that could be reframed as solvable?

What assumptions are you treating like cement that may actually be flexible and moldable?

Small shifts in mindset lead to significant shifts in outcomes. And every shift begins with this simple pivot:

Can if.

Not can't because.

Communicating Truth In A Decoupled World

I have become all things to all people so that by all possible means I might save some. I do all this for the sake of the gospel...

— 1 Corinthians 9:22-23

Communicating to a Decoupled World - a preface

By making it this far you are probably feeling two things:

Clarity & weight. Clarity around what has changed and weight around what that means for your ministry.

Although it can be a bit overwhelming, this is where the book will move toward addressing 5 key pivots ministries must make to survive this decoupled reality.

If Section One helped us see what changed, and Section Two helped us become the kind of leaders this moment requires, then Section Three answers the question every pastor eventually asks:

How do I adjust to a decoupled world, practically? How does this impact teaching and our approach to discipleship in my ministry?

Because there was a time when the average person held a more bundled framework of faith. It may not have been deeply formed, but it was coherent enough to work with:

Christian identity often implied orthodox Christian belief.
Christian belief often implied Christian practice.
Christian practice often implied church affiliation.

But we now know that layering has come apart.

Today, people assemble faith in pieces:

They may love Jesus but distrust the Church.

They may have spiritual practices but reject authority.

They may believe something is true but struggle to name what.

They may attend without committing.

Commit without submitting.

Or submit without understanding why.

Even the core dimensions of faith (identity, belief, practice, affiliation) now operate independently and form differently in each person.

Which means this:

You are no longer discipling into a shared framework.

You are addressing a room of individually assembled ones.

You can't assume what people mean by "faith."

You can't assume what they hear when you say "sin."

You can't assume what "Christian" or even "church" means to them.

This isn't just a vocabulary issue.

It's a discipleship issue.

Because discipleship begins with understanding.

And understanding begins with language.

When language loses clarity, people don't just misunderstand sermons, they misunderstand God.

So this section is not about becoming more clever.
It's about becoming more clear without becoming less compassionate or losing core convictions.

It's about learning to communicate timeless truth inside the actual lived reality people bring with them. It's about starting points and a new end point.

Not by softening the gospel.
Not by chasing cultural approval.
But by recovering the missionary instinct to meet people where they are, without leaving them where they are.

Because the gospel hasn't lost power.
But many ministries have lost touch with how people process it.

We are living in a world where belief is rarely argued into existence. It is more experienced into existence.

Identity forms relationally.
Beliefs assemble emotionally.
Practices develop socially.
Affiliation happens cautiously.

If we want to communicate truth in that environment, we must relearn how to make contact and refocus what we point people toward.

This section will help you do that.

We will explore:

- How different people enter faith through different "front doors"
- How to the think dimensionally about the faith process
- Why discipleship often begins in one dimension before reaching others
- How to preach without assuming a shared starting point
- How to rebuild language that is both clear and weighty
- How to translate without diluting
- How to hold conviction without losing connection

Because in a decoupled world, the gospel does not change.

Our entry point does.

And the leaders who will thrive in this moment will not be those who force people through old doors, but those who learn to recognize the ones God is already opening.

9: Dimensional Ministry

Week after week, we ask God to change lives.

We want hearts redirected toward Christ. We want the gospel to take root and produce lasting fruit. We want transformation, not just to give information.

And yet, if we're honest, something often feels harder than it used to be.

Not because we don't care.
Not because we haven't prayed.

But because the people sitting in front of us no longer process faith the way they once did.

Most pastors were trained to lead into a world where faith functioned as a more integrated whole. You could teach clearly from Scripture and assume people were processing from roughly the same starting point. Even if they disagreed, there was enough shared language and framework for the message to land.

That world is gone.

Today, you are teaching into a room of people whose understanding of faith has been curated in fragments shaped by algorithms, personal experience, competing narratives, and individualized belief systems.

Which means this:
Faith is processed dimensionally. People are processing faith from a particular dimension, apart from all others.

The goal of adapting our ministries is not to chase trends or keep up with culture. It is to protect the mission of transformation. Our methods should be designed to come behind what God is already doing in people's lives.

Because the gospel hasn't lost power.
But many ministries have lost touch with how people process it.

We are living in a world where belief is rarely argued into existence. It is more experienced into existence.

Identity forms relationally.
Beliefs assemble emotionally.

Practices develop socially.
Affiliation happens cautiously.

If we want to communicate truth in that environment, we must relearn how to make contact and refocus what we point people toward.

To simplify the complexity, here is the pivot: **find the dominant dimension—start there, then guide the rest.**

This applies whether you're teaching kids or adults, whether it is topical or deeply exegetical, whether it's from a stage or across a table. The issue is not your conviction about style or how you define discipleship in your ministry.

The issue is the framework you're reaching into and the assumptions you're making about how people hear what you say.

Words shift in meaning over time. It's called semantic drift.
Cultural assumptions change.
And the people sitting in front of you each week are no longer processing faith as an integrated whole.

Remember the four dimensions we've explored:
identity, beliefs, practices, and affiliations.

In a more integrated era, you could teach into one dimension and trust it could influence the others.

Address belief and identity could be influenced.
Shape practice and affiliation would reinforce it.

That's no longer how faith formation works. The people listening to you are not processing one shared message the same way. They are filtering what you say through different dimensions, at different speeds, with different questions in mind and from different echo chambers.

Which means, to communicate clearly in any manner, you are no longer giving one message to one audience. You are teaching one message to multiple frameworks, simultaneously.

And if we want our ministries to produce transformation in this environment, we must learn to operate with the dimensions in mind.

Personalizing Our Approach

Here's what I've learned:
People are far more open to change when they feel understood.

When I approach someone with genuine curiosity about where they are spiritually, conversations shift. Not because I'm more persuasive, but because I'm paying attention to where they actually are. I'm becoming more in tune with the questions they are actually asking.

I don't bring up the idea of a *decoupled network* in conversation. I simply hold it in mind. I don't mention the dimensions, I simply use them as a framework to think through.

You should too.

It gives me a quiet grid to prayerfully discern how someone is processing faith. Instead of assuming I know what someone means when they say they're a Christian, I ask questions. I listen. I try to understand which dimensions are most active for them through the questions they are asking. Are they primarily concerned about identity, beliefs, practices, or belonging?

This is a practical way I seek to come behind what God is doing in the life of someone. I can be quick to see where I think God *should* be working. But thinking dimensionally shows me where He may actually be.

Sometimes I discover a deeply integrated faith just expressed in unfamiliar language. Other times I discover real gaps that need gentle clarity. Either way, the conversation becomes more meaningful because I started with curiosity instead of assumption.

This matters enormously for ministry, especially if you teach in any capacity. If you assume everyone shares your integrated framework for faith, you will unintentionally miss parts of the room.

Not because people aren't paying attention.
Not because you weren't faithful in preparation.
But because your message isn't intersecting.

People are now hearing through different dimensions.

Some are wrestling with identity:
Who am I really? Do I even want this label?

Some are questioning belief:
Is this actually true? Can I trust Scripture? Can I trust the one using it?

Some are experimenting with practice:
What would it look like to live this out? How can I get more peace?

Some are searching for belonging before belief:
Is there a place for me here? What type of people do I want in my life?

Everyone hears the same sermon. But they do through the eyes of a dominating dimension and the questions surrounding that dimension. That complexity can feel overwhelming if we try to solve it completely.

But...

We simply need to start with awareness that multiple dimensions are present in the room. That's the trick to simplifying this overly complex decoupling of society.

This gives us a helpful grid for communication and discipleship. When people are assembling faith from fragments, they are often searching for coherence. We can then figure out where they are currently by using the dimensions as a grid and then going from there.

People are rarely as settled as they appear. A byproduct of the decoupled network is disorientation. We might not want to admit it, but when self is enthroned and reigning supreme like it does in a decoupled world, things never work out peacefully long term. So, this is why many are quietly open to clarity, guidance, and truth when it is delivered with understanding.

Which means this moment holds tremendous opportunity. Thinking dimensionally about ministry is the starting point.

When we acknowledge where people actually are, it creates connection. When people feel seen rather than managed, they listen differently. When they feel understood rather than assumed, they open more readily to transformation.

Because people rarely change when they feel managed.
They change when they feel understood.

That's the key.

Having dimensional awareness helps you connect with the desire to be known. It's not too complicated, but there is nuance in how to approach this.

Dimensional Communication

Dimensional awareness is the most practical way I've found to hold complexity with empathy. As an example, I want to introduce what I call *dimensional preaching*.

Dimensional preaching simply means preparing messages that intentionally touch all four dimensions of faith: identity, beliefs, practices, and belonging.

As I've said, if we ignore the decoupled reality, our preaching can unintentionally miss large portions of the room. When messages consistently address only one or two dimensions, people whose primary questions live elsewhere struggle to connect.

If your teaching consistently emphasizes theology or doctrine (beliefs), you may miss the person wrestling with identity. You might assume that will bleed into other dimensions, but we can no longer lead from that assumption. If your teaching tends to lean more toward the practical, you may miss the person still unsure of what they believe. You may assume the verses you are using will help shape beliefs, but that too can no longer be the assumption.

Let me explain this in a different way. These leanings we all have toward a particular dimension have assumptions about the other dimensions. By focusing heavily in one dimension you are by default neglecting the others. This means your influence is minimized.

The thing to evaluate is:
know which dimension you naturally focus on and then intentionally seek more of a balance in all four.

This doesn't mean giving equal time to each dimension in every talk or discussion. Any text or conversation will naturally emphasize some more than others. You're not forcing something artificial. You're simply expanding your preparation to consider how the text intersects with the full reality of how people process faith today.

For example, as you prepare a message or to lead a small group, four simple questions can guide you:

Identity:
How does this text speak to identity?
What does it reveal about who we are in Christ?
How might it address the question, *Who am I really?*

Beliefs:

What does this text teach about God, truth, or reality?

What theological understanding does it deepen or clarify?

How might it ground people in what is actually true?

Practices:

What does this text call us to do?

What behaviors or habits flow from it?

How does belief become visible in everyday life?

Belonging:

How does this text invite people into the community?

What does it reveal about life together as God's people?

How might it speak to someone longing for connection?

When you prepare with these dimensions in mind,[37] your message begins to land across the complexity of the room.

You won't hit everything perfectly every week.

But over time, your dimensional awareness will bring consistency in addressing people where they actually live.

---

[37] See the QR code at the end of this chapter for a chart that clearly articulates the questions and key aspects of Dimensional Discipleship.

A Simple Example

Take the Great Commission in Matthew 28 for example. The obvious emphasis is on the dimension of practice: go, make disciples, baptize, teach. But each dimension is present and can be pointed out.

Identity:

We go as representatives of the One who has all authority. Our identity is rooted in Him.

Beliefs:

Teaching assumes a body of truth worth passing on. Discipleship is grounded in what is true about God and the world.

Practices:

The command itself is deeply practical.
Go. Baptize. Teach. Make disciples.

Belonging:

"I am with you always."
The mission is communal and relational, never solitary.

You might use different wording or explain it more thoroughly. But the four dimensions are represented.

Dimensional ministry doesn't change a text, it deepens our awareness of how the text may speak to where people are. It's not asking what the passage means to different people. It's asking how a passage might reach into the faith process of a particular person.

And, we simply point it out. It's a grid that simplifies how we see the complexities of the decoupled reality.

The Goal Is Transformation

Dimensional awareness bridges gaps in discipleship created by the decoupled network because it accounts for how faith is processed today. It's not about trying to be clever. It's an effort to be a part of God's work connecting with a soul.

Scripture isn't to just be understood, it is supposed to be felt.

Yes, the Holy Spirit does the real work of change. But thoughtful preparation positions our words to land where people are listening. Ignoring the decoupled reality doesn't make it disappear. It just makes our communication less effective.

God always meets people where they are. That's our goal too. Dimensional awareness is the tool. Because when the gospel is taught in a way that connects across the core dimensions, people don't just hear it more clearly, they begin to live it more fully.

10: Transformation at the Speed of Trust

People don't grow at the speed of information.
That's important—because information moves fast.

People change at the speed of trust. And trust takes time.

This is crucial to minister effectively in a decoupled world. When identity, beliefs, practices and belonging are no longer connected, people don't simply accept what they hear. They evaluate it through the lens of who they trust.

And trust is rarely built through content alone.

Today, as we see reinforced in our research, it's built through experience and particularly in the context of relationships.

You can communicate truth with precision. You can develop a discipleship strategy. All of that matters. Faith does come from hearing, and the Spirit often uses courageous words.

But when faith is decoupled, people aren't just asking, *"Is this information true?"* They're asking, *"Can I trust where it's coming from?"*

This has profound implications.
Trust isn't built by what people finish.
It's built by someone having a track record of showing up.

This is where the tension often begins in ministry contexts. We create things for people to complete, thinking it's a key to the discipleship process. It can be a part, but relationships don't move fast. They take time and don't scale well.

And yet this is where trust is formed.
And where trust is formed, transformation follows.
This is why I say discipleship is spelled T-I-M-E.

The Mask of Content

Content is everywhere. Yet I find it both compelling and confronting to notice that transformation isn't. Ever notice that?

We live in a world overflowing with sermons, podcasts, books, and devotionals. People can access more biblical teaching in a week than most Christians would in a lifetime just a generation ago. Which strongly suggests:

Our sermons and content are no longer the unique gift our ministries offer.

We can talk about discipleship models, but the most helpful thing to recognize is that at its core, it is relational. This is why most testimonies are tied to people, not just messages. This has always been true, but especially now.

People are not following a neat, linear path of spiritual growth anymore. Their faith is fragmented, often shaped by personal experiences, questions, and circumstances they themselves can't always articulate.

Trying to address that complexity with an approach designed to have people finish a content study is like handing someone a map when they don't know where they are and don't trust the guide.

That's why relational trust is essential for transformation. And that doesn't happen on a timeline we control. Because relationships don't follow schedules. They don't move at the pace of our programs or our plans to roll out content.

Which leads to a critical pivot for mission:
Move from a content-first to a relationship-first strategy.

I know this can sound idealistic or overly romantic, like a nostalgic vision of the early church that doesn't scale. But the truth remains: transformation has always traveled at the speed of trust. And, as the research shows, trust in institutional organizations is waning.

Of course structure matters.
Programs aren't the enemy.
Teaching solid theology is critical.
We must be intentional about assimilating people.

But we cannot pretend that information alone produces formation nor can we pretend just because someone finished something we put together that they are changing. If we prioritize the efficiency of programs over the power of relationships, we may be choosing what is manageable over what is transformative.

And if relationships are the primary engine of transformation, then our strategies must reflect what we already know to be true.

Relationships Before Completion

Let me be clear: the pivot I'm proposing doesn't replace biblical content. It simply reorders it.

For recoupling to occur in the decoupled network, relationships must drive interaction with content rather than the reverse.

Instead of building studies and hoping relationships form around them, we start with how relationships form, naturally. Then content becomes the tool that serves those relationships. Not the engine that replaces them.

There are a few reasons this matters.

First, belonging is always discovered through relationships, not attendance. Participating and finishing something we put together can be a starting point, but we also know you can attend something for years and still feel like an outsider. You can attend and then go back to your life.

Second, younger generations are increasingly looking for belonging outside the church walls. If your ministry fails to help people cultivate meaningful connection outside of your organized programming, they will find it somewhere else.

This means relational proximity matters more than ever. The question really is: are we willing to meet people where they seek connection or will we stay stuck trying to get them to come to something we want them to finish?

People locate themselves through relationships.

So although a curriculum may provide some structure, from a shepherding perspective, we know it is through consistent relationships that we can actually meet people where they are.

A Relational Infrastructure

This can be a pretty big shift when you think about it. It can feel extremely ambiguous, like some nostalgic home church ideal.

So, let's step back and look at the bigger picture before getting into specific implications. First, a relational starting place would change the initial question we ask.

Instead of asking, *"What content should our small groups go through?"* you might consider asking, *"How can we encourage our people to live relationally?"*

That question alone begins to shift thinking about methods.

Most pointedly, it moves us to including qualitative metrics. From programmatic metrics to including relational ones.

What I've learned about church settings is that most requests for groups are a request for relational facilitation. People want friends. And the more we facilitate it within the church the less people have friendships outside the church. Things always become more insular...and thus, less transformative.

And, even though we may not think about it, this is where the mission erodes. Trust in institutionalized churches has been eroding is tied to how our programming naturally turns the relational connections of people more insular. Acknowledging how this may impact the mission is critical.

Canvas Church in Kalispell, Montana is a helpful example. It is a "mega-church" by any standard, but lead pastor Kevin Geer understands the importance of relationships and their church is seeing tremendous fruit because of it.

Several years ago, they made a significant pivot in how they approached discipleship. They completely removed their life groups. Not because they didn't value community, but because they wanted to prioritize it differently.

Instead of organizing people into groups built around content or a designed schedule, they began encouraging a model centered on relationships. The ones that were already in place. The ones people already had.

Their mindset was simple: *We preach to help people live.*

That clarity changed everything. Rather than asking people to join something new that was organized by the church, they began encouraging people to live intentionally within the relationships they already had. Family. Friends. Coworkers. Neighbors.

This meant they stopped organizing relationships for people. They refer to this as *incarnational living*—bringing faith into everyday relationships rather than isolating it inside church organized structures.

Internally, they describe it as a *transformational model,* built around three relational spheres:

- Church friends
- Jesus friends (people walking closely with Christ)
- Lost friends (people not yet following Jesus)

They often visualize this as a Venn diagram, where life is ideally lived in the overlap of those relationships. The goal isn't to separate them, it's to see people move toward the middle where they all overlap evenly.

They also measure how this is going. They survey their congregation around the relational spheres. Kevin will teach for 10 minutes and the rest of the service is solely focused on everyone taking a survey that asks questions like:

- Who do you spend the most time with?
- Who are you investing in spiritually?
- Who are you connected to outside the church?

This is a great example of reframing discipleship for the decoupled network because it's directly connected to how trust is naturally built. In and through relationships. And here's the thing: people have them already.

For Canvas Church it's no longer about getting people into the right group or having them finish a set process. It's about helping people live the right kind of life within the relationships they already have. That's the critical pivot point.

And while they can support people by pointing them toward helpful content, they've intentionally moved away from cultivating what they call "content-rich groups" toward emphasizing "life-rich relationships."

Because of that, much of the relational work has been owned by the people themselves. Part of spiritual development, in their view, is simply learning how to live with, love, and navigate real relationships over time.

So, in other words, they don't organize relationships for people. In fact, Kevin is known for often saying to the church, *"We aren't a Tinder app for you to find friends."*

You might be surprised to know the results have been significant. This doesn't just require less staff and less budget, there is real quantitative data that supports this approach.

Before this shift, Canvas Church averaged around 250 baptisms a year. However, in the last two years, after changing their methods to a relationship-first approach, that number has grown to over 630 annually. They are seeing the fruits of a relationally focused approach to mission... and it is quantifiable.

They are trusting God to use His people, relationally. They built a relational infrastructure of metrics that aligns with how people actually grow and how trust is actually formed in life today.

Most pointedly, their relationship-first approach has helped them build trust with people outside the faith. And the baptisms prove it.

Transformational Metrics

Now, I understand that not everyone is at a place to stop their current model. Canvas Church has obviously cultivated a change-ready culture to pull that off. That said, if they can change their entire approach... you can change *something*.

So let's talk about a starting place.

From a leadership perspective, instead of measuring discipleship by program attendance alone, begin by asking some specific questions. A data-informed decision is needed in this area so, consider running an anonymous survey to better understand this.

Ask people if they feel known.

Ask if they have spiritual friendships.

Ask how many relationships they have with non-believers.

Ask if they think anyone would notice if they quietly drifted away.

The goal is not more activity. The priority is that we are ensuring programs serve relationships rather than masking their absence.

Sign-ups are measurable. Full rooms feel like progress. We feel a sense of control and accomplishment when participation is high. But we have to remember that attendance doesn't mean influence anymore.

Although having a content-first approach can give us a sense of control, we know we can't police what is actually taught in a group. We can't control what people absorb. We can't manufacture spiritual formation.

This leads to some more questions that must be addressed.

If success isn't based on what people finish, what am I actually measuring? Where is trust actually being built in my ministry rather than assumed? Is our model built for efficiency or transformation? Where might our current "success" be masking shallow formation? Are our people truly engaging with people outside of our church?

As a ministry, success is to be measured more by who our people are becoming. Attendance matters. Giving matters. Serving matters. These are good and necessary metrics. They just aren't enough.

We must expand what we measure to include relational depth and evidence of formation. Are people growing in how they love? Are they known by others? Do they practice repentance? Are they being challenged and cared for? Are they becoming more like Christ in observable ways? Are they engaging with the world around them?

This doesn't require massive structural overhaul, at least not immediately. Small adjustments can begin in the questions we ask. Moving toward relationally driven metrics that help discern whether transformation is actually taking place.

Because if we measure only what's easy to count, we may miss what actually counts.

Priesthood Of All

The pool of leaders can feel like it shrinks quickly when we start thinking relationally about discipleship. It can seem harder to develop leaders who can shepherd people toward Scripture through real relationships rather than structured programs.

But we must be careful to not underestimate the power of God working through His people. God's people are His choice for ministry. And yet, if we are not careful, as leaders we can allow our desire for control to limit God's work through them.

It can feel risky at first. But you can start small with a few people you trust to do some very simple things.

Invite a college student to lunch after church.
Host people for the Super Bowl.
Have a young couple over for dinner.

You're not asking people to try or change everything.
 Just something.

Most people already have relationships forming naturally. The opportunity is to be more intentional about what God is already doing through them and doing so outside the church walls. Canvas Church may be an extreme example from a structural perspective, but it is a good one to keep in mind. If they can change as a large ministry, everyone else can at least take small steps.

What if your strategy was to simply ask a few people this question: can you get to the point where a few people know where every dish is in your kitchen?

Better yet, you might ask: who already knows where every dish is in your kitchen?

And then, you help them realize that's the starting place. Articulate this as them already embracing incarnational living.

Think about what would have to be true for that to happen. Think about the conversations. The trust earned. The shared meals. The amount of life lived together. The questions sifted through in order to know where every dish is.

That kind of relational depth doesn't require a budget.
It doesn't require staff.
It doesn't require a new program.
No staff management required.

It only requires a pivot of intentionality toward how we all know transformation works. At the speed of trust.

The hope behind a relationship-first model is simple: God works through His people. When believers walk together, share honestly, struggle openly, and live in proximity, the Spirit moves. Lives change.

The harder part, if we're honest, is trusting God to work through people rather than through what we organize.

So, here is one thing to keep in mind: people may need extensive training to run a program in your ministry. But to invite someone into their home? Not so much. To start with the relationships they already have? That's easy.

Actually, when you think about it this way the pool of potential leaders actually expands, dramatically. Because, now you're working with the priesthood of all believers.

No single model is superior to another. This is simply about honoring how God has always worked through people, in relationships, over time.

Relationships don't fit neatly on spreadsheets. They can't be programmed or predicted. No one wants their friendships structured for them. Real connection happens slowly, at the pace trust allows. But everyone is already connected in some form.

That's why the pivot is clear:

encourage discipleship around relational infrastructure first, and let content come alongside when helpful.

Because transformation begins with proximity. How you do that will vary, but putting relationships first must be the priority.

Making The Pivot Practical

Regardless of how ambiguous this may feel, there are at least four practical steps you can begin taking. The key is to move toward where people are, even if it is incrementally.

First, if your culture is largely built around content, you might begin just by building pathways that specifically address each of the four dimensions: identity, beliefs, practices, and belonging. This may include studies or classes, but the key is intentionality. When you name the dimensions clearly, you increase your chances of addressing the questions people are actually asking, not just the content *you think* might be good.

Second, begin tracking relational and transformational metrics. Not to create a scorecard, but to gain clarity. To do this you need feedback loops. Things like a survey, small group leader observations or pastoral and mentor check-ins can be considered. But you are looking for feedback on both vertical and horizontal markers of growth. Vertical indicators might include things like:

- consistency in prayer
- engagement with Scripture
- rhythms of confession and repentance
- growth in the fruit of the Spirit
- generosity and trust in God

- rhythm of life commitments

Horizontal indicators might include:

- meaningful faith conversations
- serving and community involvement
- helping someone else grow spiritually
- relational balance with believers and non-believers
- relational reconciliation stories
- freedom from addiction

You're not looking for perfect data.
You're looking for directional clarity.

Are people changing? Do they have a sense of relational connection? Or just attending?

Third, design environments for engagement, not just consumption. Create spaces off your church campus whenever possible where people can process, ask questions, and wrestle honestly. Passive listening rarely produces transformation. People long for safe places to explore faith with others they trust.

Courses like Alpha, discussion environments, or simple hosted gatherings can create space for real conversation. When people feel safe to process, they begin to open. When they open, transformation is much more plausible.

Fourth, define your language clearly. Ask ten people to define "spiritual growth" and you'll likely get ten different answers. So working with your team to clarify what you mean when you use words like discipleship, evangelism, maturity, and formation is more important than ever.

People don't grow in confusion. They grow in clarity.

All of this leads to one core evaluation: *Are we measuring attendance or transformation?*

In a decoupled reality we must ask very honest questions about our methods: Is this actually producing change and keeping us on mission or is this program simply maintaining itself?

Not every program needs to be eliminated. But without evaluation, programs stop serving the mission and slowly become it.

If what we're doing isn't producing transformation, it isn't succeeding, no matter how efficient it looks on a spreadsheet.

This includes the words we choose.
That is where we turn next.

11: The Art of Ostranenie

False teaching is a concern.

But there is another issue that is just as dangerous in preaching. It's subversive, which might even make it more dangerous and it's something that we rarely think about.

It's *familiar* teaching.

I'm talking about when we repeat sacred truths so much that they become background noise.

The words are still true.
But they're no longer heard.

Because when something becomes too familiar, it stops being felt. And when truth is no longer felt, transformation is rare.

This is why every leader needs to understand a concept called, *Ostranenie* (awe-strah-nee-nee).

Keeping Meaning Alive

In the early 1900s, a Russian literary critic named Viktor Shklovsky introduced a concept called *Ostranenie*. The idea is simple: when something becomes overly familiar, we stop noticing it. We stop feeling it. We stop being moved by it.

Embracing this reality, writers and artists began intentionally presenting familiar things in unfamiliar ways so people could experience them again. That's the art of Ostranenie.

They called this *defamiliarization* and the goal was to keep the meaning of something alive.

The goal of this art wasn't to be novel.
It was to preserve the importance of something.

When something is reframed just enough, people see it again.
Hear it again.
Feel it again.

Ministries desperately needs this.

Not because the truth has changed.
But because everyone is in vocabulary ruts and sometimes people have heard it so often that it becomes like wallpaper. It's there, but nobody pays attention to it anymore.

Sacred words can become hollow sounds if we're not careful.
Holy vocabulary can turn into background noise.
When this happens, truths can lose their weight.

This causes transformation to slow and why this matters.

Don't get me wrong, scripture still has the same power. The Spirit still does the same work.

But the fact remains: people stop noticing what they think they already know.

The Real Threat

One of the great threats to leaders today is assuming people understand the weight of words they use.

But vocabulary ruts—where we are saying the same sacred things the same way, can actually create the opposite effect. Because it's familiar, people think they understand, and once that happens, listeners mentally file away what you're saying before it ever reaches their heart.

They don't reject the message.
They pre-categorize it.

They assume they know where you're going. They assume they've heard it before. So they stop listening.

The words can still be true. But they no longer interrupt
anything because, when truth becomes predictable, it stops
feeling personal.

This is especially true for the decoupled network. In a world
where people already live inside fragmented attention and
endless content. Familiar church language often lands like static
in a noisy environment. Not offensive. Just ignorable.

And ignored truth doesn't transform.
So, the way we talk about truth matters.

Jesus Did This Constantly

Jesus used this art of Ostranenie all the time to defamiliarize
people from the truth he was presenting.

Parables were a form of it.

He took familiar experiences like farming, fishing, family
conflict, lost coins and used them to reframe how people saw
God, the Kingdom, and themselves. People came expecting one
thing and left with their categories rearranged.

He just changed angles on truth by defamiliarizing its context.

This art helped people finally see what had always been there.
It just hadn't landed.

That's the heart of this chapter.

Not clever preaching. Not edgy communication.
The goal is providing fresh sight into timeless truth through all
we do and say in our ministries.

The Prism Mindset

Think of Scripture like light passing through a prism.

The light doesn't change.
But when you turn the prism, new colors appear. You gain a fresh
perspective on the light each turn.

That's what effective teaching does.
Same truth.
Just a different angle.
Fresh clarity.

Ostranenie is simply learning how to turn the prism.

It's presenting familiar truth from an angle that interrupts
automatic hearing and helps people feel it again.

Not for creativity's sake.
For transformation's sake.

Because every ministry lives inside familiar vocabulary. Words like:

Salvation.
Discipleship.
Grace.
Worship.
Community.
Sin.
Evangelism.

People have heard these words for years, sometimes decades. Many can predict what you're going to say about them before you say it. Once they believe they know, they stop listening.

It's not resistance to truth.
It's overexposure to how you talk about it.

But, it's interesting to think about because if you were to ask them to define the word, they may not be able to. Or, you may get as many definitions as people in the room. That's because when language becomes predictable, it becomes weightless. When it becomes weightless, it becomes ignorable. And when it becomes ignorable, transformation slows.

In a decoupled world, this matters even more.

People are approaching identity, belief, practice, and belonging from different angles and at different speeds. That means familiar church language often misses where they actually live.

It's not a matter of truth missing.

It's more about how we start our conversation about the truth we want them to feel.

Turning the Prism With Dimensions

This is where dimensional awareness can become a powerful tool for your communication.

Identity. Belief. Practice. Affiliation.

These dimensions function like a second prism. They help us take familiar theological language and turn it just enough that people can see it again.

Same truth. New angle so what we say can be delivered in a way that lands with how people process faith today.

This is the pivot: **use the dimensions as a form of defamiliarization to creatively reframe familiar truths.**

For instance, take the word *discipleship*.

For many people, it sounds like a program: Bible studies, small groups, serving teams, accountability, spiritual disciplines. All good things. But for many listeners, the word itself has become too familiar to feel meaningful.

Leaders can say they want to *make disciples who make disciples*. But many people won't even know what that means. It's just using a familiar word twice.

This is where you can turn the prism by using the dimensions as a grid for how you talk about it. Consider these examples of how you might do this:

Identity: Christianity is less about what we do and more about who we're becoming.
Belief: Christianity is learning to trust what Jesus says is true—even when it challenges what we feel is true.
Practice: The Christian life is about training our lives into new rhythms, not just gaining knowledge.
Belonging: Growth happens in relationships, not isolation.

Same idea, just a reframing through the dimensions. Using the dimensions to help clearly define common words you use will cause familiar language to be felt again.

Or take the word *worship*.

Many people immediately think of singing. Music styles. Preferences. Experiences. Over time, worship can become a consumer moment instead of a formative one and this can be reinforced weekly in how we talk about it. From the stage, when we say things like, we are going "into a time of worship" it impacts how people think about the word. What it actually communicates is leaving your life behind so you can now enter something different called "worship." We all know worship is not music, but these vocabulary ruts can not only steer people toward wrongful thinking, they can also become so familiar that nobody hears them anymore.

Consider turning the prism dimensionally.

Identity: Worship reminds us who God says we are before it asks what we sing.

Belief: What we are about to sing will declare what's true even when our emotions say otherwise.

Practice: Worship forms habits that move us out of the center so we can fully focus on the Lord's presence and the fact that He hears us.

Belonging: Worship is a "we" word, speaking of a people gathered around the One who gathers us.

Same truth.

New potential for clarity.

Or consider one last example: *sin.* This is one of the most misunderstood words in modern culture. When handled poorly, it lands like a moral lecture. Behavior management. Shame.

Now, turn the dimensional prism.

Identity: Sin disforms who you were created to be.
Belief: Sin is self-destructive betrayal of a relationship with God.
Practice: Sin is a habit of misdirected love that slowly steers us away from freedom.
Belonging: Sin isolates us from God and those He wants in our lives.

Here sin becomes more of a diagnosis, instead of an accusation. It can bring clarity without cruelty, which is what the gospel of grace does.

You may use different words, but turning the prism is the point.

Translation Without Compromise

The power of dimensional defamiliarization is simple:
It helps people hear the truth again without having to change it.

You don't soften the gospel.
You don't dilute conviction.

You change the angle so people can see through the framework they are operating from already.

When people can't connect with our language, they often assume they can't connect with our faith. They don't reject Jesus first. They tune out vocabulary they can't locate themselves inside.

Words like *saved, discipleship, sanctification,* and *community* can begin to feel like insider language. Not because people haven't heard them, but because they've heard them so often they no longer know what they mean.

Defamiliarization helps restore meaning and dimensional awareness helps you navigate that.

It helps people feel what they've heard. See what they've overlooked. Engage what they've ignored...becasue it meets them where they are.

The Goal

So, Ostranenie is about helping people experience truth again.

Fresh sight into timeless truth.
Clarity without compromise.
Familiar words that feel personal again.

In today's world, this may be one of the most important shifts ministry leaders can make — taking intentional time to articulate timeless truths to a decoupled reality.

Here's a secret:

it can actually reignite things for you personally too!

Embracing the idea of Ostranenie by using the dimensions to reframe what has become familiar can help you and others see again. Feel again. Hear again.

Using this dimensional approach inherently communicates a posture that says:

I see you.
I understand the complexity.
I know how you're processing.

And when people feel seen, they lean in. When they lean in, truth more likely lands. When truth lands, transformation begins.

That's the goal.
Not novelty.
Not cleverness.
Not catchy phrasing.

Fresh sight into timeless truth. We never want to try changing the message. We are just trying to help people hear it afresh.

And that's why I say the art of Ostranenie may be one of the most important tools for the future of ministry — especially as it points them to the cross.

I'll explain why next.

12: A Sharper Center

The term *gospel* is used in a number of different ways. While it can be a term that people are over familiarized with, it is still an important word.

Vital, in fact.
But in a self-curated reality the weight of it can be lost.

The problem isn't that we've stopped teaching the truth.
It's more that people have lost the center of it.

People don't need more religious information or language. They need a gospel to confront self, the focal point of the decoupled network.

This means we need a sharper center. A foundational centerpiece. And that center is not "faith in general," not "spirituality," not even "Jesus" in the abstract. I would argue it's what Paul called the supreme thing:

"We are determined to know nothing among you
except Jesus Christ and him crucified."
—1 Corinthians 2:2

That line is easy to quote but even easier to overlook. Paul isn't making a clever theological statement. He's describing a determination. A decision and a calling to every individual who desires to follow Jesus. It's the ground from which everything else grows.

It's known as *terroir* in the wine industry. A trained person can taste a particular wine and then identify the specific soil the grape came from. The grown grape points to a particular topography. This is something the decoupling of faith has caused the Church to lose in culture. Instead of pointing to the cross, everything now points back to the individual self.

The crucifixion provides much needed grounding and it wasn't merely Paul's preaching preference. It was his anchor. He chose to know Jesus relationally, but through a specific lens:

the cross.

Notice Paul doesn't say, "except Jesus Christ and the fact that he died." He is specific about the manner: he was crucified.

Like Paul, the cross can no longer just be a topic in our discipleship. It must become the lens through which we view ministry. The interpretive center of how we understand God, humanity, sin, salvation, and discipleship. The center to which our very lives should point to.

The cross is strong enough to undermine an enthroned self.

So, this is a call back to where the anchor clings to unwavering ground. A resetting of our center into orthodoxy where the cross isn't just spoken of in the context of forgiveness, but worship. A clear, specific, and unapologetic center. It's not a model or method. It's a re-centering of all we do and believe.

The cross didn't just inform Paul's message. It structured his theology, his worship, his leadership, and his understanding of human nature.

This is the pivot to consider: **recenter the cross as the primary picture of discipleship.**

Whether we realize it or not, every era emphasizes certain aspects of the gospel. And our era is no different. In a decoupled world where self sits enthroned, the cross is not optional. It is the center strong enough to hold firm.

Changes In Gospel Emphasis

It's important to note that the Church's dominant articulation of the gospel has always shifted by era, context, and audience.

That's not a compromise. It's an understanding of what it takes
to stay on mission.

Across church history, the church didn't try to change the gospel.
But it often emphasized different angles of it. The prism kept
turning based on what people most needed to hear.

Christ's death has always been central (e.g. Paul saying "Jesus
Christ and him crucified"). But how his death was communicated
has varied. It has shifted from victory, sacrifice, substitution,
healing, and liberation.

There's overlap in every era. But clear patterns emerge.

In the early church (1st–4th centuries), people lived in a pagan,
polytheistic world filled with fear of spirits and death. So the
church proclaimed Jesus as Lord. Preaching emphasized Christ's
victory, the resurrection, and using Kingdom language. What
tended to land most clearly was how Christ defeated the powers
and offered new life.

In the Medieval world (5th–15th centuries), identity was
inherited, belonging was communal, and life was framed around
cosmic order. The gospel was often articulated relationally,
emphasizing union with Christ, healing, restoration, formation.
The emphasis was on how Christ fixes what is broken.

During the Reformation, the church leaned into courtroom language. Sin as guilt. God as Judge. Christ as substitute. This framing spoke directly to spiritual anxiety in a system where salvation was largely mediated through the Roman Catholic Church. The gospel was articulated as justification by personal faith, Christ standing in our place.

In the Great Awakenings (18th–19th centuries), the emphasis shifted again. Frontier expansion, social upheaval, and moral reform movements created a need for personal response. Preaching became more individualistic, calling people to make a personal decision. Revivalism and altar calls emerged in that context.

From the 1940s through the 1990s, the gospel was often articulated around personal relationships: Jesus died for your sins, you can now accept Him into your heart and grow through discipleship. This resonated in a culture shaped by individualism, suburban expansion, and a longing for stability after war. Language like "God loves you" and "you can know Him personally" became dominant.

In our current era (2000 to the present), articulation has shifted again. Identity language, trauma, shame, healing, justice, and belonging now shape how people hear the gospel. Compassion language matters. Community matters. Apologetics often come through pointing to beauty, story, and lived experience. This resonates in a culture shaped by distrust, therapy frameworks, and deep fragmentation.

It's the same gospel. But the entry points the Church utilized most have changed. That is good missionary work.

Why This Matters

The Church has always adjusted how it articulates the gospel. Jesus' death remained central, but the doorway into the message kept shifting. Each era reframed the gospel in language people needed to hear at the time, pointing people to it through language they understood.

That overview (which was admittedly over simplified) reveals something important: every generation required a fresh articulation. Not new truth, just renewed clarity.

And today's cultural center is not pagan fear, inherited identity, institutional authority, or moral reform. It's the reigning of self, cemented like never before. Self as authority. Self as interpreter. Self as savior.

Which is why the cross must be resurfaced in a way that directly confronts this centering.

In a decoupled world, where the dimensions are all processed independently through echo chambers curated to serve self, the cross speaks with unique precision. It exposes the illusion that we can construct faith on our own terms, like an a la carte buffet where we decide what *we* want.

It confronts self-salvation at its root.
It confronts the refusal to submit to the truth.
Every era needs a faithful and refreshed articulation.

And for this moment, the focus on Christ crucified is not just relevant. It is not only helpful. It is necessary.

The Decoupled Center: Self

Let's take a deeper look at why resurfacing the cross in our communication might be the most faithful and effective response to a decoupled reality.

Self-centeredness has always been a core issue. Selfishness has never needed to be taught. But the decoupled self is manifesting uniquely from the rest of history.

What happens when people feel free to mix, match, and manage each dimension on their own terms?

People decide for themselves what "Christian" means (identity), which doctrines should matter (belief), which rhythms they'll adopt (practice), and where, if anywhere, they'll belong (affiliation).

At first glance, this can look harmless, even thoughtful. It feels personal. Nuanced. It can be seen as mature or as someone taking responsibility for their own faith.

But look closer.

Self is quietly sitting at the center of it all.

I decide.
I choose.
I curate.

I opt in. I opt out.
I build a faith that fits me.

That isn't discipleship.
That's self-direction dressed up as spiritual maturity.

It's a mindset that assumes: *I design how this works.*

And that's why life inside a decoupled mindset can struggle to produce deep, lasting, biblical faith. Because biblical faith is not built on self-expression. It's built on self-forgetfulness.

Surrender. On receiving versus curating for ourselves.

Yes, this all reflects an echo-chamber world. But it is also, in part, the unintended fruit of how the church has spoken about the gospel over time.

Language like, "grow in your personal relationship with God" came from a good place. It pushed against a system where faith was mediated through institutions and reclaimed personal access to Christ.

But over time, the emphasis subtly shifted.

Christianity became framed as primarily *me and God*, rather than Paul's focus on Christ and His cross. Personal experience became the anchor. The individual became the interpreter of truth and fellowship with other believers became an option. We have even emphasized everyone being like "a Berean," deciding for themselves what is true or not.

Everything becomes about getting to know ourselves better and knowing what serves us best. Things like Strength Finders or the Enneagram, as good and helpful as they may be, begin to dominate. Because, understanding and serving oneself becomes the goal.

Knowing who we are and having a strong sense of self-awareness is necessary. But what do you get when self becomes the center?

Everything becomes optional. Belief becomes negotiable. Practice becomes preference. Belonging becomes temporary. Authority becomes internal.

At that point, we don't just need better explanations. We need a stronger center.

That's why the cross must return to the middle. Because God's choice of utilizing the cross confronts self in a way nothing else can.

It refuses our illusion of control. It exposes our true need. And it recenters faith where it has always belonged. Not in us, but in the self-giving love of Christ and Him crucified.

Why Preaching "Jesus" Isn't Enough

I have to say this plainly: You can preach about Jesus and still miss the gospel.

Many sermons speak about Jesus but never truly center on the crucifixion. His death and resurrection get mentioned, but often as background information rather than the interpretive key to everything else being said.

But we cannot talk about the person of Jesus without talking about what he did on the cross. It's not just critical to understanding forgiveness, it's critical to understanding who Jesus is and who we are.

Because his obedience on the cross reveals everything.

It exposes the severity of our sin.
It shows the depth of God's love.
It gives definition to the nature of salvation.
And it confronts the real problem: self-centeredness.

You can preach "Jesus" in a way that actually supports self-centered faith.

Jesus as life coach.
Jesus as guide.
Jesus as comforter.

Jesus as therapist.

Jesus as wisdom teacher.

And yes, Jesus is compassionate.

He is near.

He is tender with the broken.

He is our friend.

But if the cross is not central, people won't embrace him as Savior. They'll meet him as an accessory to the life they're already trying to build. Yet we know that doesn't work.

And if someone doesn't recognize their need to be saved, Jesus ultimately has nothing to offer them.

Because that's who he is.

The Savior.

Which means the cross isn't just the entry point to Christianity. It's the clearest diagnosis of the human condition. It cuts straight through our self-centeredness and exposes the deepest issue needing to be addressed beneath the surface.

It's not culture.

Not politics.

Not technology.

It's self-expression over self-forgetfulness.

And until self is confronted head on, the gospel will always feel optional to those that hear it.

Humanity's Mistress

There's a reason Paul didn't say, "we preach Christ died."
He said, "we preach Christ crucified."

That's far more pointed. It gives us a sharper center for understanding the self-giving love of God, what Jesus has done, and how believing in him reshapes our lives.

The cross isn't just the fact of his death.
It's the meaning of that death.

It's the collision point where humanity's selfishness and God's self-giving love met in public.

And in that moment, the truth Scripture has always declared is exposed: we are not basically good, not spiritually neutral, not merely misguided.

We are lost.

And our lostness has a powerful guide: Self.

The cross reveals what I call humanity's mistress. It's the thing
we keep returning to, protecting, feeding, and quietly defending
beneath everything else.

Me.
My rights.
My preferences.
My comfort.
My control.
My autonomy.
My identity as I define it.
My truth.
My way.

Self is the operating system of a decoupled network.

Which is why Christ's selfless acts on the cross cannot be
optional in our teaching.

To a decoupled world, the cross is like seasoning is to meat. The
entire gospel tastes different when it becomes the focal point.
Without it, people can absorb Christian ideas and still remain
self-centered. With it, the self-centered life is exposed,
confronted, and invited into something entirely new.

Because the cross does not renovate the self.
The cross points the self toward death.

This allows identity to be received, beliefs to be submissive, practices to become worship and affiliation to be familial.

The crucifixion preaches uniquely to a non-submissive decoupled network because: it's much easier to submit to the teachings of someone who chose that manner of death over every other possibility.

The cross is key to recoupling what the world has torn apart. We will look more deeply into that next.

13: The Cross Recouples

One of the most powerful effects of having the cross resurface as a pillar in our ministry is that it reshapes the Church into a confessional community.

I don't mean confessional in the sense of theological camps or drawing denominational lines.

I mean confessional in the sense of truth-telling.

A group of people who can say, together:

"We cannot save ourselves"
"We cannot make ourselves whole."
"We cannot heal what is broken in us."

And that type of confession meets its companion most clearly at the cross.

For Paul, the cross was never an intellectual fixation. It was a spiritual strategy. He knew something we often forget:

The cross is not merely the symbol of how we are saved.
It is the central teaching point for how to live.

The cross amplifies God's self-giving love — why we worship.
The cross amplifies God's self-forgetfulness — how we live.

In other words, the cross is the lens through which we hear everything Jesus taught for what it means to follow him.

If theology is the Church's teaching, the cross is the guidepost that helps us relate to it all.

And its power lies in what it does at the same time.

The cross confronts our sin by amplifying God's love.

It declares:

"You are more sinful than you want to admit.
And more loved than you can comprehend."

As my friend Josh White often says, "Even on your worst day, God is crazy about you." Nothing reveals that more clearly than the cross. It is the place where we are confronted by a love we could never earn.

So the cross is more than sentiment. It is love expressed through sacrifice. It is the saving act of Christ, not just for individuals, but for the reconciliation of the world.

The cross screams: no matter how far your sin goes, God's love goes deeper and further.

And when people truly see that, when the cross is preached with clarity and weight, something begins to happen.

Faith starts a re-coupling process because the cross reorders everything. When the cross becomes our guidepost:

Identity becomes received, not curated.
Beliefs become submissive, not negotiated.
Practices become worship, not preference.
Affiliation becomes family, not convenience.

Death No Longer Has the Final Word

The cross speaks one more thing everyone needs to hear:

What feels final is not.

The cross reminds us that death no longer has the last word. Yes, we preach resurrection. Yes, we proclaim victory.

But the empty tomb is not detached optimism.
It is hope purchased.

The cross was the cost.
The resurrection was the payoff.

Without the sacrifice of Christ at the center, the decoupled self is left to feed on its own strength, its own meaning, its own story.

But the cross interrupts that under a different narrative. It highlights the saving act of Christ. The doorway through which resurrection life enters.

Which means we never preach the cross as tragedy alone. We preach it as triumph disguised as defeat.

And when people truly see it, their self-authored story begins to unravel. They are confronted with a reality they would never write for themselves, a love they could not produce and a rescue they could not engineer.

And that realization doesn't crush hope.

It awakens it.

Because the cross declares that even in our darkest moment, even in what feels final, God was already writing the story of redemption.

This frees the decoupled self from its own bondage. Here is a way of looking at this:

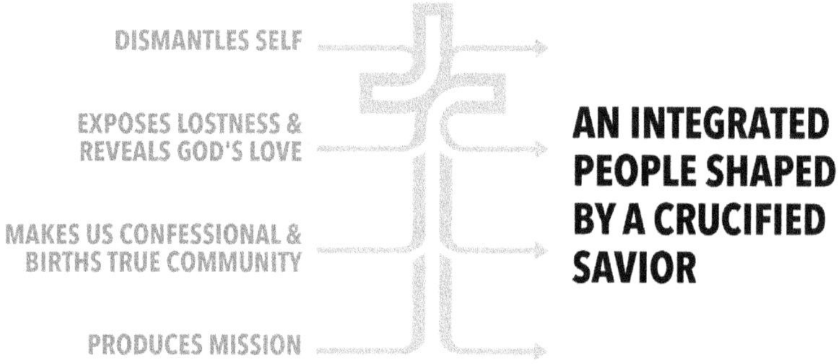

Informed Living

The cross doesn't just explain how we are saved.
It shapes how we think and live as followers of Jesus.

To understand the cross is to be formed by it. And a cross-formed life cannot leave the self on the throne.

This is where self-denial becomes essential. It's not an optional discipline, but the starting posture of discipleship.

Jesus didn't say, "Follow me by improving yourself."
He didn't say, "Follow me by getting your life more organized."

He said, "Deny yourself, take up your cross, and follow me."

Self-denial comes before following.
This is not an advanced step of Christianity.

It is Christianity.

And this matters because much of modern spiritual formation focuses on habits, rhythms, and practices. These are helpful things, very good things, but when it becomes about self improvement we easily skip the one posture Jesus made foundational:

Self-denial.
Why is this so crucial?

Because the decoupled world enthrones the self, the gospel centers on Christ, and the bridge between those two worlds is the cross.

It's the ultimate picture of self-forgetfulness.

And understanding Christ's act on the cross does not simply forgive the self.

It dethrones it.

The Cross That Reconnects

When the cross returns to the center, everything begins to make sense again.

It reinterprets everything for us.

The cross defines who we are (identity).
It reveals God's love most clearly (belief).
It shapes a life that takes self out of the center (practice).
It gathers us into a confessional people (affiliation).

It doesn't mean every bible study becomes a crucifixion talk.
It means everything best lands through the lens of the cross.

THE CROSS RE-COUPLES

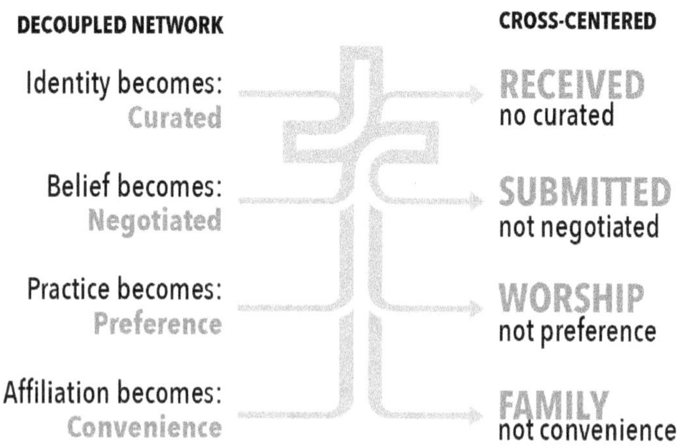

Because the cross dismantles the self,

the center of the decoupled world.

The cross exposes our lostness,

which the decoupled self hides.

The cross reveals God's love,

which the decoupled self redirects inward.

The cross forms confession,

which the decoupled self resists.

The cross births community,

which the decoupled self treats as optional.

The cross ignites mission,

which the decoupled self reduces to self-improvement.

That's what cross-centered faith produces:

A recoupled faith shaped by a crucified Savior.

The world offers self-improvement.

The gospel offers self-denial that leads to resurrection life.

That's the message to a self-reinforcing echo chamber world.

That's the invitation to the decoupled network.

That's what transforms a fragmented people.

Because when Christ crucified is central, self-centered faith
becomes impossible.

And that is exactly what the world needs today.[38]

A Communication Grid

So now the question becomes:
How do we communicate the cross in a way people can actually hear without compromising the message?

How do we teach it across generations?
Across different starting points?

Let me close this chapter by offering a simple framework for re-centering the cross in your teaching and discipleship.

Not as a formula. Just a guide.

1. Expose the Decoupled Self

"Who's at the center?"

Cross-centered teaching begins with clarity.

In an era of re-forming, most people share one assumption:
I decide.
I decide what Christianity means to me.

---

[38] See QR code at the end of the chapter for more on dimensional teaching grids, examples of how cross-centered preaching applies to different generations or Trinitarian preaching to a decoupled world.

I decide which beliefs matter.

I decide what I practice.

I decide where I belong.

The problem isn't that people have questions.

The problem is that self sits on the throne while they ask them.

So the starting point is exposure. Who's at the center?

This isn't to shame.

Instead the goal is to awaken.

Because until self is exposed, the gospel feels optional.

Jesus might be seen as helpful, but faith becomes self-serving.

And people remain stuck trying to save themselves.

2. Name the Problem Clearly

"Self is a cruel savior."

You cannot preach the cross without naming the disease it heals.

The core issue of the Re-formation age is not confusion.

It's not politics.

Not culture.

It is idolatry.

Self is a cruel savior.

Self demands constant performance.

Self feeds anxiety.

Self breeds isolation.

Self makes commitment conditional and discipleship optional.

A word of caution here: we must avoid turning this into a rant about some sort of culture war where we point out how culture is off base. The cross doesn't point outward first.

It points inward.
Toward the mistress we all constantly defend: self.

3. Proclaim the Cross

"Christ did what we cannot."

Now comes the good news.

We cannot preach "Jesus" in vague terms.
We must preach what He did and why.

Because the decoupled world does not need vague spirituality.
It needs rescue.

The cross declares a clear message:
Someone else did for you what you could never do for yourself.

You cannot save yourself through identity.

You cannot redeem yourself through better beliefs.

You cannot heal yourself through better practices.

You cannot belong your way into righteousness.

Christ crucified is the end of self-salvation.

The collapse of performance.

The announcement that grace is real.

The cross is fixed as central to the message.

But people's entry points are not.

This is why you might consider how different generations often hear through different doors. Each generation has a general lens they see the world through. This means we can hone in how we talk about the freedom Christ provides with intentionality:

- Boomers: guilt → forgiveness and assurance
- Gen X: meaning → truth without spin
- Millennials: shame → love and restoration
- Gen Z: fear → rescue and belonging

Again, we understand it's the same cross, the same gospel. Just different words that lead to different front doors.

The dimensions are a helpful grid as well, but your job as shepherd and teacher is to prayerfully discern which door helps your people hear the clearest.

4. Invite Confession

"You don't need improvement. You need rescue."

Confession is where the gospel becomes personal.
Not surface agreement. Not admiration. Not vocabulary.

Confession.

The Church becomes powerful again when it becomes a
confessional people who can say:

I need mercy.
I cannot carry my sin.
I cannot heal myself.
I cannot be my own savior.

In a decoupled age, one of the most important things a pastor
can do is move people from curating their own faith to
confessing their need. This is the only point where identity
becomes received, beliefs become submitted, practices become
worship that crystalize into belonging to a family.

The bottom line is: if we don't recognize our need for saving,
Jesus really has nothing to offer us.

He is the Savior. This is why you might consider making efforts
to provide times of prayer and confession for your people. It

meets the relational needs of our fragmented world, it addresses the mask of an echo chamber world where people hide behind screens, and it points us to honest confession that helps build relational trust.

5. Call to a Cross-Shaped Life

"Self-denial is the doorway to life."

The cross doesn't just point us toward forgiveness.
It forms our perceptions of what it means to follow Jesus.

As we have seen, the decoupled web enthrones the self.
The gospel récenters Christ in a much needed way.

Self-denial is not God shrinking us. It is God freeing us and that's a major difference.

Taking ourselves out of the center in no way ends our life.
It is truly the beginning of it. The cross points to just that.

6. Offer Belonging

"The cross makes a people, not just believers."

Decoupling fragments our sense of belonging.

Many believe without belonging.

Consume sermons but avoid community.

Hold private faith but reject public commitment.

Understanding the cross never leads us to isolation. It forms us into being a substantial part of a people.

A confessional people. A forgiven people. A humble and courageous people.

The cross doesn't just save individuals.
It forms a family.

How to Use This Grid

As you prepare to teach, consider asking:

- Did I expose self at the center?
- Did I name self as a cruel savior?
- Did I proclaim Christ crucified clearly?
- Did I invite confession?
- Did I call people to surrender versus self-improvement?
- Did I offer belonging over independence?

Then ask one more question:

Which doorway helps my people hear the cross best?
Guilt? Shame? Fear? Meaning?

That's not a compromise. That's a loving way to provide clarity that can lead to a recoupling of a disoriented decoupled person.

Because the Church cannot afford teaching people merely consume. We need teaching that confronts self by centering the acts of Christ on the cross.

That's the kind of ministry that doesn't just pass along content. God often uses it to awaken.

Use the QR code to download the
free resources mentioned in this chapter.

14: On-ramp Connections

Most sermons start with the idea that Scripture is going to be the authoritative source for the message. That used to work.

It doesn't really anymore.
I know that sounds bad, possibly even heretical.

But I don't mean that because Scripture has lost authority. I mean it because many people have never granted it the authority it deserves. And when they don't respect its authority, they will shut it out of what they hear.

So, there's a strategic question every preacher and teacher now has to wrestle with:

If every sermon must land at the cross...what's the on-ramp to that if scripture has lost its rightful authoritative seat?

We've talked about reframing familiar topics. We've explored how centering the cross helps recouple what has come apart.

We've looked at dimensional ministry and applying Scripture across identity, belief, practice, and belonging.

But here's the reality sitting underneath all of it:

Scripture is losing authority in the lives of people, and even among believers.

We cannot ignore this.

Reestablishing the authority of Scripture is not a side task.
It is central for ministry in a Re-forming era.

In a previous generation, you could begin with Scripture and assume people place some trust in it. You could quote a verse and expect it to settle the matter, at least to some degree.

The Bible says it so that should be enough.
That provided the authority.

That assumption no longer holds for many of the people we're trying to reach. Barna research shows that in 2025 only 42% of self-professing Christians strongly affirm that the Bible is "totally accurate in all of the principles it teaches."

This is not a reason to abandon Scripture.
It is not a call to soften biblical preaching.
Scripture is authoritative.

Always has been.
Always will be.

This is a call to be honest about the landscape we are preaching into. When you speak to others who don't already accept biblical authority, beginning with "the Bible says..." can create distance before connection.

Not because people are hostile toward the Bible, but because they don't yet have a framework for why it should matter. This creates barriers that take work and intentionality to overcome.

Starting with something they haven't bought into and expecting immediate obedience doesn't make sense.

If the cross is where we must land, we have to think carefully about where we start.

Today vs. Yesterday

One common instinct is to defend Scripture by proving its accuracy: historically, geographically, textually. To explain how well it's been preserved. To show how it surpasses other ancient documents in reliability.

Those conversations matter.
They're true.
They still have a place.

But in many ways…

Those are yesterday's questions, not today's.

That approach speaks most clearly to older generations formed in a truth-first world. They can ask those questions.

Today, many people, especially younger generations, begin somewhere else entirely. Many believe moral right and wrong can change over time. Individual belief becomes the basis for moral judgment. Truth is not assumed to be objective or fixed.

And, as we've seen, younger generations often care less about whether something is objectively true than they do about whether it is good.

That distinction matters. Because it means we're often answering truth questions while people are asking value questions. The value questions are what need to be answered.

The pivot to consider is this: **start with shared values, then lead to Scripture as their source and the cross as the landing place.**

There are certain values almost everyone affirms, regardless of belief. Things like integrity, kindness, justice, generosity, stewardship, compassion and legacy.

These resonate because they tap into something deeply human.

When you begin here, you meet people where they already are.
You establish common ground.
You demonstrate how what you're teaching connects to what they already care about.

And from that ground, you lead deeper.

You show how those values reflect the heart of God.
How Scripture has always pointed toward them.
How the cross becomes their clearest expression.
How Jesus' model of them can reform how we think about them.

You connect their existing intuitions to a truth that both clarifies and transforms them, personally.

This isn't bait-and-switch. You're not pretending to talk about one thing while aiming at another.

You're starting with real common ground and building toward deeper truth.

Paul did this in Acts 17 at the Areopagus. He didn't begin with Hebrew Scripture because his audience didn't accept its authority. Instead, he started with what they already valued. He referenced their altar to an unknown god. He quoted their poets. He connected with their search for meaning.

And from there, he led them to resurrection.

It was strategic.

Confrontational yet somehow relational.

Intentional.

Even if his audience didn't agree, they felt seen. He met them where they were and built a bridge to where they needed to go. We need that same kind of thinking now.

In a decoupled mindset where authority is not assumed beyond self, we must work harder to build bridges. We can't simply assert conclusions and expect people to follow. God can use anything, but faithful ministry must be intentional.

We should never use God's sovereignty as an excuse for our laziness.

Value Based Starting Points

Here's how this might work practically.

Take generosity. You could begin with: "The Bible commands us to be generous." But for many people, it may be interesting but not compelling.

Or you could begin somewhere else.

Meaning.

Legacy.

Freedom.

Anxiety.

Most people want their lives to count. They want their resources
to matter. They want something beyond consumption.

We all know we can't take money with us.
But we can direct it toward what outlasts us.

You can talk about how most people don't actually want more
stuff. Most simply want more freedom, a sense of meaning. Yet
debt, lifestyle pressure, and constant consumption quietly
control their lives. We work to pay for things we thought would
make us happy.

Generosity interrupts that cycle.
It loosens money's grip.
It reminds us we are more than consumers.

Or maybe you consider starting with anxiety.

Money is one of the biggest sources of fear in our culture: having
enough, keeping enough, not losing what we've built.

But what if generosity isn't about losing security...but finding it?

People who live generously often experience less fear because
their trust shifts from what they control to something deeper —

God's provision. Over time, they learn security isn't something they build, it's something they receive.

Or another idea is to begin with identity.

Many assume churches talk about money because churches need it. While that can be true, generosity is not primarily about funding an institution. It's about forming a person.

Every financial decision shapes who we're becoming. Generosity trains us away from self-centered living and toward open-handed trust.

There are countless entry points and you can discern which ones fit best. That may be depending on your context or timing. The key is to start with something that is commonly defined as a good thing.

But the pattern holds:
Start with what people value. Then pivot toward scripture with phrases like:

"...And this is exactly where Scripture meets us. Long before cultural reflection or modern research, the Bible spoke directly to this..."

It gives the opportunity for Scripture to land differently.

Not as a disconnected and imposed rule.
But as revealed wisdom on the values they hold.

By the time you talk about tithing, it no longer feels like an arbitrary religious requirement. It becomes a practice that makes sense, a rhythm designed for freedom, trust, and joy.

Starting with common values does a few things well.

It: honors what people already care about, connects faith to real life, and prepares hearts to hear Scripture with clarity and authority.

It doesn't replace biblical teaching.
It prepares people to receive it.

And when self reigns supreme, that matters.

Because when Scripture is approached this way, it no longer feels distant or imposed. It feels like the source of what people were searching for all along.

And that's where recoupling begins.
This is part of how we avoid trying to solve the complexities of our moment and instead shepherd people through it.

Door To The Gospel

This approach often takes more time. It's easier to quote verses, make pronouncements, or talk about giving the same way you always have. But we've already seen how people block out what is familiar.

Plus, easier rarely equals effective. And the goal isn't information transfer. It's not just obedience. It's transformation. That means this kind of preparation is worth the time and thought.

This doesn't just shape preaching. It shapes evangelism and everyday discipleship conversations.

This doesn't just work from the pulpit. When you're talking with anyone who doesn't share your faith, you don't have to begin with theological propositions. Shared human experience is usually much more effective.

No one makes it to adulthood whole.
Everyone wants to be loved.
Everyone wrestles with meaning.
Everyone faces death and wonders if their life mattered.
Everyone has been hurt and longs for trusting relationships.

These are human universals. And the gospel speaks directly to them, to every aspect we desire.

Intimacy. Meaning. Pleasure.[39]

As I stated in the introduction, when people don't know how these fit together, a kind of weariness sets in that sleep doesn't fix. People feel disoriented. They don't know where to locate themselves in the story of their own lives.

These aren't abstract topics. They're front-of-mind for nearly everyone and touch every dimension of faith: identity, belief, practice, and belonging.

When we start here, we speak a language people already understand. We show that faith is not disconnected from real life. We demonstrate that the gospel addresses what actually keeps people up at night.

From that common ground, we can move naturally toward the work of Christ. Rather than jumping directly to the call of carrying the cross of Christ...
We can present the gospel as the answer to the questions people are already carrying.

The risk of skipping this step is simple: we end up answering questions no one is asking.

---

[39] For a Dimensional Discipleship Guide for these topics (including how they apply across generations) see the QR code at the end of this chapter.

And when that happens, people don't reject the gospel, they just disconnect from it. It's okay to preach the gospel and trust God to work through whatever we say. It's also okay to be attuned to who is in front of us so we can make the presentation as personal as possible.

This is why beginning with common ground matters. It isn't a compromise. It isn't avoiding the truth. It isn't softening the claims of Scripture.

It's engaging, strategically. It's an understanding of the mission.

We are seeking to meet people where they are, clearly guiding them toward where they need to go: Into a transformative union with a triune God.

And, the best and clearest on-ramp for a transformative dialogue is finding common ground and using common language.

**Use the QR code to download the
free resources mentioned in this chapter.**

15. Pivot Now

You didn't pick this moment.

You didn't ask for a culture that shifts faster than your sermon series or your small group calendar. You didn't design a world where discipleship is no longer linear, where identity, belief, practice, and belonging no longer move together.

But this is the moment you've been entrusted with.

And that means the question in front of you isn't whether change is coming. Change is already here.

It's happening in your congregation. It's happening in your community. It's also happening within you.

Like we said at the beginning—change is always the same. It is constant. It creates tension. It forces us to decide what we hold onto and what we release.

So the real question is this:

What if the greatest threat to our ministries isn't change... but staying the same?

That question isn't meant to create panic.
It's meant to create clarity.

Because ministries don't drift because culture shifts. They drift because leadership stops responding to it.

And that rarely happens all at once. It happens slowly. Quietly. One decision at a time. Through comfort. Through familiarity. Through the subtle shift of preserving methods while assuming the mission will somehow carry on without them.

But it won't. Not because the mission is fragile, but because the mission requires movement.

Mission Outlasts Methods

One of the hardest realities for any leader to face is this:

Ministries rarely decline because they lost the mission.
They decline because they stopped adapting how they pursue it.

And often, that happens in the name of caring for the people already in our ministries. Of course this isn't all bad.

But it can be if we just protect what feels familiar. We preserve what once worked. We assume that holding onto methods is the same as holding onto faithfulness.

But there is a difference between holding the line and losing the plot.

The line we hold is not our structure. It's not our schedule. It's not the programs we use. The line we hold is the gospel. And the mission that the gospel proclaims.

This whole time, I've used the phrase "our mission." It's even in the subtitle of this book. But the truth is... it's not really ours.

The eleven apostles were commissioned. This is more than semantics.
From a missiological view, God's mission has a Church.

And what we've been invited into is far bigger than any model, method, or ministry structure we've built.

The gospel has endured empires, exiles, awakenings, migrations, persecutions, pandemics, and technological revolutions.
Through every cultural shift, one thing has remained true:

God's mission endured.
The Church adapted.
And the kingdom advanced.

So if you find yourself clinging to methods simply because they are familiar, hear this with pastoral urgency:

You may not be protecting the mission.
You may be burying it in your context.

And I say that carefully. Not as a critique—but as a call.

A call to pause. To reflect. To ask God for clarity.

Because this matters.

Familiarity Is Not Faithfulness

This book has circled around one hard truth in many ways:

The greatest danger for church leaders today is not heresy.
It's numbness.

It's the slow drift into routines that no longer form people, even though they once did.

We can do ministry on autopilot and call it faithfulness.
We can reuse language and call it clarity.
We can preserve systems and call it stewardship.

But here is both the warning and the invitation:
Faithfulness is obedience to God's mission in the moment you've been given. And that requires courage.

Not loud, performative courage.
But steady, Spirit-led courage.

The kind that keeps you anchored when things feel uncertain. The kind that allows you to move forward even when not everyone understands.

Because courageous leadership doesn't just proclaim truth. It carries truth—relationally, patiently, faithfully—into changing terrain.

Courageous Leadership in a Decoupled World

A decoupled world requires a different kind of shepherding.

You can no longer assume shared language. You can no longer assume shared beliefs. You can no longer assume people know what they believe... or who they are.

And you cannot solve that by simply adding more content.

Content matters.
Theology matters.
Teaching matters.

But without trust, those things become weightless.

Heard... but not trusted. Received... but not integrated.

Which is why your leadership must become:
More anchored—not anxious.
More courageous—not more defensive.
More missionary—not more appeasing.

And courage here is not about personality. It's about conviction. Conviction that God's mission will outlast the methods you love. Conviction that change is not a threat—it's a tool. Conviction that adapting how we lead can actually protect what matters most.

Truth Is Non-Negotiable. Articulation Is Not.

This is what mature leadership understands.

We hold firmly to the truth. We hold loosely to how we communicate it. The gospel does not change.

But the way people hear it does.

And refusing to adapt how we communicate truth isn't always faithfulness. Sometimes it's just a refusal to learn the language of the people we're called to reach.

You are not compromising the truth when you clarify it. You are not watering down the gospel when you translate it. You are not abandoning tradition when you stop idolizing methods.

The gospel is not fragile. It does not depend on a particular delivery system to remain powerful.

But it does require us to proclaim it like it's alive. Like it matters. Like it's for this moment.

Because it is.

What Pivoting Really Means

Pivoting is not panic. It's not novelty. It's not chasing trends.

Pivoting is missionary leadership. It's the willingness to ask:

What endures?
What is re-forming?
What do we need to change?

It's the humility to study your context as carefully as you study Scripture. Because you are not just called to preach truth. You are called to preach truth to real people, in a real place, at a real time.

Pivoting is the courage to say: We will not preserve what is comfortable if it costs us what is faithful.

It's evaluating everything through the lens of transformation—not just participation.

Asking: Is this forming people? Or is it just maintaining itself?

Because if you don't evaluate your systems, they won't serve the mission. They will slowly become it.

You Are Not Alone

Let me speak to you as a pastor. Leading change is heavy. It is emotionally demanding, spiritually stretching, and certainly carries relational complexities.

If you've made it this far, you likely feel that weight.

And I want you to know that feeling is not a sign that something is wrong. It's a sign that you care. But you must also acknowledge the harsh realities that are coming your way.

You will be misunderstood. You will be questioned. You will second-guess yourself at times.

Other moments you may feel like you're the only one that believes in what you are doing.

You will feel the pull to go back to what feels safe—especially when resistance rises and you get tired.

But you were not called to preserve comfort. You were called to carry the mission. And you are not alone in that calling.

God is with you.

The same Christ who is building His Church is not asking you to carry it on your own. You are not the Savior of your church.

Jesus is.

Which means you are free.

Free to lead with courage.
Free to make decisions.
Free to adapt when needed.

Not because you'll always get it right...but because your confidence is rooted in God's faithfulness, not your perfection.

The Cross Remains the Center

If change is the landscape, then the cross is the compass. If culture is shifting, then Christ crucified is your anchor. If people are decoupling their faith, then the cross is what brings it back together.

Paul didn't say this as a strategy. He said it as conviction:

"We are determined to know nothing among you except Jesus Christ and Him crucified."

Because the cross confronts self. It calls for surrender. It invites people into rescue. And it forms a people.

No matter how much the world changes, this remains true:

The cross still speaks. The cross still confronts self like nothing else could. Keep it at the center, and every pivot will strengthen the mission.

A Final Invitation

This book is meant to be an invitation.

An invitation to lead with courage. To move with clarity. To honor the past without being bound by it. To act without waiting for perfect certainty.

Because there is a cost to delay. A cost to indecision, comfort and to staying the same. But there is also an opportunity.

An opportunity to lead your ministry into its next season with faith, humility, and boldness. Or, possibly to hand it off to someone who will.

So let me ask you to consider the question again: What if the greatest threat to your ministry isn't change—but staying the same?

If that's true, then the most faithful thing you can do is not preserve what worked yesterday...but pursue what the mission requires today. To at very least evaluate the methods you are using through the lens of transformation rather than the comfort of those leading them.

God's mission will outlast the methods we love. So hold tightly to the mission. And hold loosely to the methods.

You are not managing an institution. You are stewarding people.

People God loves.
People God is calling.
People God wants to transform.

This is your moment. Not later.
It's time to embrace your call: Pivot Now.